Boris Becker's Tennis

The making of a champion

Boris Breskvar
in collaboration with Ulrich Kaiser

 SBL Springfield Books Limited

I would like to take this opportunity to thank all the friends who persuaded me to write this book; without their active help and support it would never have been written.

Boris Breskvar

Photo credits

Adidas, Herzogenaurach 82
Baden Tennis Association, Leimen 6
Lorenz Bader, Munich 11, 53, 65, 76/77, 92
Becker 66 (3), 94, 108
Thomas Exler Production, Olching-Esting 23 (8), 25, 29 (7), 42 (6), 43 (3), 45, 58, 106/107, 127
German Press Agency (DPA), Frankfurt 37 (Wattenberg), 60/61 (Schrader)
Laci Legenstein 112
Mosaik Verlag (Michael Steinke) 10, 16 (4), 17, 22 (6), 28 (6), 30 (6), 34 (6), 35 (6), 39 (6), 49 (6), 50 (2), 51 (4), 52 (6), 54 (2), 55 (4), 56 (6), 57 (6), 62 (6), 63 (6), 114, 116, 128
PUMA Photo by Paul Zimmer 13, 17, 19, 36
Hans Rauchensteiner, Munich 84
Sven Simon, Essen 2/3, 14, 38, 120, 124
Völkl, Herzogenaurach 110
Bernd Wende, Berlin 80, 122
Paul Zimmer, Stuttgart 8, 18, 19, 20 (5), 21, 26, 27, 31, 32/33, 40/41, 44, 46/47, 48 (2), 50, 59 (2), 67, 68, 71, 79, 81, 84, 86 (2), 87, 89, 90, 91, 95, 100, 105, 123

Acknowledgements

Illustrations: Heinz Bogner
Cover design: Douglas Martin Associates
Design and layout: Paul Wollweber/Douglas Martin Associates
Front cover photo: Sven Simon
Back cover photo: Baden Tennis Association, Leimen
Translation: Andrew Shackleton/Alder Translation Services
Technical adviser on English edition: Charles Applewhaite, Director of Coaching, Lawn Tennis Association

Printed in Germany by Mohndruck Graphische Betriebe GmbH

ISBN: 0 947655 23 9·

Original text copyright © 1985 Mosaik Verlag GmbH, Munich/54321, West Germany

English translation copyright © 1987 Springfield Books Limited, Springfield House, Norman Road, Denby Dale, Huddersfield HD8 8TH, West Yorkshire, Great Britain

Breskvar, Boris
  Boris Becker's tennis : the making of a champion.
  1. Tennis
  I. Title II. Kaiser, Ulrich III. Tennis wie es Boris Becker bei mir lernte. *English*
  796.342'2   GV995

Contents

Foreword 7

Spotting talent 9

> **A perfectly normal boy 12**

Survey of techniques – pros and cons 15
Holding the racket 15
Forehand grip 15 – Backhand grip 16 – Semi-continental grip 16 – Double-handed backhand grip 16
The ready position 17
Footwork 18
Stationary shots 19 – Shots on the move 19 – Jumping shots 20 – Different strokes 20
The forehand 21
Forehand topspin 24 – Forehand slice 24

> **Leimen 26**

The backhand 25
Backhand topspin 29 – Backhand slice 30
The volley 31
Forehand volley 31 – Backhand volley 35

> **An example to follow 37**

The service 38
The return of serve 44
The smash 48
The backhand smash 50
The lob 51

> **Hair colour 53**

The dropshot 54
The drop volley 54
The half volley 55
The double-handed backhand 57
Surprise shots 59
Which strokes for which players? 62

> **The development of talent 66**

Training for competition 69

> **Typical training weeks for Boris Becker 70**

Specific forms of physical training 70
Coordination training 70 – Reaction training 72 – Training ball sense 72 – Ranger training 72 – Stretching programmes 72 – Strength programmes 72 – Endurance training 74 – Special exercises for Steffi and Boris 79

> **The importance of conviction 82**

Training the mind 81
The psychology of training and competition 81 – Relaxation exercises 84 – Mental rehearsal 85 – Improving aggression 86 – Concentration training 88 – Coping with stress 89

> **Self-confidence 87**

> **A born competitor 90**

The match 93
Preparation 93
Psychology 93 – Strategy 94 – Warm-up 95
Tactics 95
Singles 95 – Doubles 101 – Psychological tactics 104

Tennis for older players 111

Equipment 115
The racket 115 – The strings 116 – The ball 117 – How do experts string their rackets? 118

Adapting to different kinds of court 121

Injuries and their prevention 125

> **Boris Breskvar, the coach 128**

Foreword

In the summer of 1985, while still overwhelmed by his rise to fame at the age of only seventeen, Boris Becker spent one of his rare quiet moments talking unprompted about his first coach, Boris Breskvar. He had started training with him at the age of six, at about the same time as he had started school. But whereas he could hardly remember his first day at school, he could recall every detail of his first lesson with Breskvar. For it was Breskvar who taught him to play tennis – not, perhaps, the game he plays all over the world today, but the basic building blocks of the game without which a top-class sporting career would have been quite impossible.

Boris didn't just mean learning how to develop the right stroke or the right shot. Rather, he recalled the countless extra lessons and training, the patience of his coach – and no doubt the impatience of a pupil for whom nothing could happen quickly enough. Perhaps he was also thinking of how he had really enjoyed what for others had merely been a hard grind, and that it was all thanks to Boris Breskvar that he still found pleasure in training. He also commented that Breskvar had always played tennis with him man to man – we all know how good it feels for a youngster to be treated like an adult. Boris Becker was not quite fifteen when he played against senior players to become the youngest-ever German champion. It was about the same time that Breskvar first lost to his pupil.

This book by Boris Breskvar is no mere flash in the pan, knocked off in a hurry because the opportunity suddenly presented itself. In this book, he not only presents all the techniques and refinements of top-class tennis, but also recognises the importance of the right teaching methods, both for children and for adults. He concentrates on the progress of the individual player in terms of style and achievement towards the best that he or she is capable of. It is this approach, in which careful direction is more important than strict adherence to a set programme of exercises, which has since made the Sports College in Leimen into a breeding ground for champions. Boris Becker said that without Boris Breskvar he could never have achieved his high ambitions. What better tribute could a coach wish to receive?

Ulrich Kaiser

Spotting talent

What is it that makes a tennis champion? It's not just a matter of physical characteristics. There are, for example, players who are barely five foot seven tall but have still achieved world-class tennis, while others have managed it at six foot three. They have simply played a different style of game.

One might also ask what is the earliest age at which talent can be recognised. Like other sports, tennis has seen a dramatic lowering of the age at which high performance levels are achieved. Among the men it began with Björn Borg, who was succeeded by Stefan Edberg from Sweden, Aaron Krickstein from America, and of course Boris Becker himself. Among the women it was Chris Evert who set the ball rolling, to be followed by Tracy Austin, Andrea Jaeger, Gabriella Sabatini from Argentina, and of course Steffi Graf. They have all proved that even in the 15–17 age range it is possible to move into world-class tennis.

I am of course fully aware of the counter-arguments which emphasise the dangers of high-performance sport at such a young age, and I don't wish to ignore them. However, it is my opinion that the cases of harm to young performers which have been cited in support of these arguments reveal a number of mistakes in training. In cases where talent for the game has been stifled or has simply evaporated, the causes, whether psychological or physical, can usually be attributed to the people surrounding the teenager concerned. Bad periodisation of the training programme, and an overloaded timetable in the interests of competition, can lead to damage which is often irreparable. The young player may lose all interest and enjoyment in the game, and his growing body may even be physically damaged by inappropriate training.

Faulty training plans usually involve specialisation at too early a stage. If a child plays nothing but tennis, day in, day out, then boredom eventually creeps in. Even unconscious resistance may in the long run have a negative effect. I therefore lay great emphasis on a varied training programme, interspersed with suitable rest phases (see **The development of talent** on page 66).

A talent for sport generally is not sufficient to produce a good tennis player, though it is clearly useful if the player is good at ball sports. Everyone can think of people who have achieved incredible skill in whatever ball sport they have played, whether football, handball or basketball, or even hockey, golf

The signs of a future tennis player manifest themselves very early on

or billiards. They can cope with anything provided it is round! In the case of tennis, however, there are many other abilities which can be expected to produce success if present in the right combination. These are coordination, dexterity, speed, learning ability, motivation, willpower, concentration, stability, the willingness to take risks, self-reliance and unflagging optimism.

This list may seem discouraging at first sight, but if you think about it it is quite logical. Someone who is successful at a particular sport will often look rather out of place in a different kind of sport. The reasons for this are obvious. A swimmer, for example, needs a completely different kind of body coordination from a tennis player, and certainly doesn't require any ball sense. The swimmer cannot see his competitors, and this results in a completely different psychological approach to the sport. He has no need to try to surprise or outwit the other competitors, for example. Lastly, swimming requires a totally different combination of motor abilities.

My own work provides a marvellous example of this. People often send outstanding runners to me on the basis that a good runner also makes a good tennis player. Now footwork is important in tennis, but it is only one requirement among many. The only thing that running on a court has in common with running on a track is that both are done with the legs. In all these years I can't remember a single outstanding young runner or athlete who has turned into a really good tennis player. In most cases it is ball sense that is lacking. On the

Talented children can develop amazing athletic skills from a very young age

other hand, I have only rarely been disappointed by good handball, football or basketball players. They already have a feeling for the ball, irrespective of whether it is leather, rubber, fibrous or whatever. Call it talent, heredity or what you like – they have it!

These are just some of the things you need to be aware of if you want to spot a gifted tennis player early on. My assistants and I have always made our first observations by getting children to play tennis against each other. But this is not sufficient on its own. It is obvious that those who have had the most training will play the best tennis at first, since they will know what you need to do to keep the ball in the game.

More important than this is the impression that a young boy or girl makes when the coach plays a ball to them so that it is as awkward as possible to hit. I might, for example, keep trying to catch the young person on the wrong foot. This will tend to highlight certain important

traits which are indicative of future development: coordination, dexterity and fighting spirit. How good a player really is can be seen from the way he reacts to such difficult situations. In my opinion the most important requirements for a good tennis player are agility, coordination and speed in converting thought into action.

The next test is not quite as simple as it might appear. I get the children to throw a tennis ball as far as they can from the base line. This gives an idea of a player's coordination and the muscular power in the shoulders – both vital elements for producing a good service.

The children then have to hit a series of lobs and drop shots, which is the easiest way of assessing a player's ball sense – a factor which is limited in the degree to which it can be trained.

Finally, we play a few games

which might seem to have very little to do with tennis, such as football, hockey and especially basketball. Watching these carefully quickly reveals several of the abilities already mentioned – and more: body coordination, dexterity, the desire to win, tactical ability, willingness to take risks, concentration and aggression.

If you record all your observations on these various activities, collate them and assess them all together, you will obtain a clear picture of a player's talent – or lack of it.

I vividly remember the routine screening of children carried out by the Baden Tennis Association in 1974 and 1975, for this was when Boris Becker and Steffi Graf were first introduced to me. I was immediately struck by little Boris – though not by his technique, which was then not so much bad as non-existent. This was quite understandable since at that stage he had done no more than play on his own against a wall. What impressed me was his fighting spirit, his coordination and especially his incredible ball sense.

If I shot the ball left and right into the corners to try and catch him on the wrong foot, he would use every means in his power to reach the ball and send it back. As a last resort he would even then throw himself to the ground like a goalkeeper. Only he had no notion of how to roll over, and would graze his elbows and knees in the process. I had never seen a boy with such enormous willpower and commitment.

I immediately started to give him regular training. The first thing I did was something I had never tried

with any other pupil before: I taught him to dive and roll properly – because I wanted to keep him in one piece! If he insisted on playing tennis that way, then at least he should do it correctly. These days, when I watch him carry out this spectacular manoeuvre, and note that his subconscious reactions are exactly right, then I can't help thinking back to those first lessons.

With Steffi Graf it was a completely different story. She was only six when she first came to us, but she already had a fairly reasonable technique. She had learned the basics from her father, who was a tennis coach. I can clearly recall the first time we met. Peter Graf came up to me and said, "I've found out as much as I can

about you, and I think you're the right man to train Steffi – because one day she's going to be number one in the world!" I don't think I could have been blamed for assuming that I was talking to yet another of these ambitious fathers who think the whole world is just waiting to see their child play. Anybody else would have thought exactly the same. But I very quickly had to revise my opinion of him. By the time we had completed the half-hour training session I was greatly impressed, and inwardly asked Peter Graf to forgive me for thinking so ill of him. For Steffi really did have talent.

If a player has talent this will be particularly obvious in difficult situations

A perfectly normal boy

We sometimes forget that the 19-year-old Wimbledon champion has not always been the self-confident young man who stormed to victory with his massive tennis shots. Boris was once a boy just like any other – rather cheeky, sometimes worried, sometimes shy – in short, a bit of a rascal at times!

Before going to training camp in Yugoslavia, he was repeatedly warned to behave properly and not to make trouble. So he stayed in his room long after all the others had escaped for the evening, the reason being that he had brought his favourite honey and marmalade with him, which had attracted whole armies of ants. He wanted to keep this quiet for fear of being sent home, and so he wasn't released from his imprisonment until someone eventually went up to his room and found the poor lad hiding there surrounded by hoards of insects.

On another occasion some of the older players very much wanted to go to a disco, so they sent him to plead on their behalf. He kept on begging, protesting that it was his own idea, until they eventually gave in and let them go on condition that they were back in by ten. But when they arrived at the disco, they were stopped by the bouncer; the 18-year-olds were allowed in, but not so the fair-haired young lad, because he was only 14. So poor Boris had to wait outside for three or four hours, until the others came out and he could go back with them.

Boris was always being teased by the other players because he worked so hard at his game and never let up. And at 13 he was by far the youngest competitor in the German Youth Championships. You know what it's like when lads of 17 or 18 want to assert their superiority over a boy of only 13 or 14. They expect him to show "respect" – always calling them "sir", standing up for them, and even giving up his seat for them. But Boris found ways of getting his own back. One evening he was hanging round the court reserved for the 18-year-olds, where one of his tormentors was playing. It was already 9 o'clock, so someone suggested he went to bed. He grumbled a bit at first. But then he stood up obediently, and called down to his "friend" on the court, who was concentrating hard on his service. "Hi there, Rolf!" he shouted. Rolf stopped and looked up at the rostrum, his concentration gone. Boris waved and called again: "Just wanted to tell you I'm off now! Bye! See you tomorrow!"

Once a brand new video camera had been installed at enormous expense in one of the courts at the training centre, only to be wrenched from its wall socket by a ball hit by Boris with incredible force. The camera was still working, but the poor lad was dreadfully upset. He had to be reassured that it wasn't his fault. He had merely done what had been required of him, and no one could have foreseen such a hard shot from a lad of his age!

He was 15 when it came to the attention of a sports equipment firm that he had managed to destroy nearly a dozen of their most expensive rackets within the space of three months! An inquiry was held, and the Adidas man came in person to reassure himself that nothing untoward was going on.

Another time he was treated to a giant helping of spaghetti by a girl five years older than him. He came back to thank her next day, blushing with embarrassment and carrying a bouquet of flowers. "The flowers are from my mother!" he explained.

But what is so special about all these events? They are, after all, no different from the harmless exploits of any lad of that age. And perhaps it is that "lad-next-door" quality about Boris that has endeared him to the public all over the world.

Even on Centre Court there were football interludes for the Queen – typical Boris!

Survey of techniques – pros and cons

Holding the racket

Ever since our ancestors first hit on the idea of using a racket to put a ball over a net, there have been disagreements as to the correct way of holding the racket. It is essential to grip the racket correctly if you are to hit the ball properly with a good smooth stroke, but in my opinion the best grip depends very much on the player's physical make-up; it will vary from one individual to another. This is certainly true of world-class players, who all hold their rackets slightly differently for each of the various shots. This is quite simply because each player has found the position for each stroke which is exactly right for him.

Finding the best racket position as early as possible is vital for success; it will be a long and difficult task to change the position later on. Unfamiliarity with the new position will make it feel very strange and uncomfortable at first. This in turn will have an adverse effect on your confidence and hence on your performance; after all, no one is pleased if he suddenly loses to someone he has previously always beaten. This understandably tempts you to return to the old familiar racket position. But there is no other solution than to come to terms with

this temporary setback if you are eventually to improve.

Therefore a player who finds he is holding his racket in an unsuitable position must consider carefully whether it is really worth the effort of correcting his grip. It is a lot easier for children to make such changes than for adults. Old habits die very hard.

Forehand grip

The basic rule is this: try to hold the racket in such a way that you can hit the ball at the right point in relation to your body, and can make the most efficient use of the muscular power involved. The easiest way to find this position is as follows: place yourself sideways to the net and hold the neck of the racket with your left hand, keeping your left arm outstretched and making sure that the head of the racket is vertical. Now bring your right hand towards the grip from the right and take hold of the grip. (All these directions should be taken the opposite way round if you are left-handed.)

At the same time make sure that the base of the little finger goes just as far as the end of the handle and no further, and that the index finger is slightly splayed. This allows you to retain the necessary degree of

The road to the mastery of special techniques is a long one

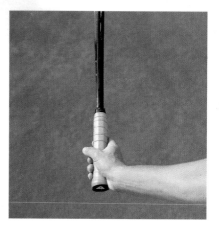

Eastern grip

flexibility in the wrist. This particular grip is known as the *eastern grip*.

If you keep the head of the racket vertical and let your right hand approach the grip from a point below and to the right of the handle, this will produce what is known as the *western grip*. Here again, the base of the little finger should just reach the end of the grip, though for anatomical reasons the index finger will not be as splayed. This particular grip is especially common among players who hit the ball with a lot of topspin – a technique which Björn Borg has made very popular.

There are of course countless variations on these two types of grip, involving fine adjustments of the hand position. It is worth experimenting to find exactly the right forehand grip for each individual player.

Backhand grip
The backhand grip is also known as the *continental grip*, and the simplest way to find it is as follows. Keep the head of the racket vertical and approach the grip from above. The base of the little finger should again touch the end of the grip, but in this case it will rest on the top of the grip. The thumb should point forwards and downwards along the left side of the grip. Players who prefer to use a lot of topspin will often turn the hand slightly further to the left – a position known as the *extreme continental grip*.

The continental grip can also be used for the service and for the smash.

Semi-continental grip
The position known as the semi-continental grip is produced as follows. Keep the head of the racket vertical and bring the right hand towards the grip from a point above and to the right of the grip. The base of the little finger should again touch the end of the grip, and will rest on the angled surface to

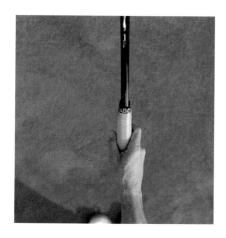

Semi-continental grip

the right of the top of the grip. This grip can be used for the volley, the service and the smash, as well as for the forehand or backhand slice.

Double-handed backhand grip
The double-handed backhand has been much despised in the past, but in the last ten years it has become more popular, as many world-class players have used it to great effect. They have often continued to use this particular grip – once dismissed as a bad habit – simply because they used it as children at a time when the racket

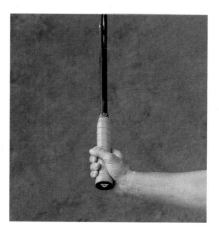

Western grip

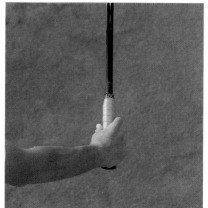

Continental grip

Double-handed backhand grip

was really too heavy for them.

The right hand holds the racket using the continental grip, while the left hand is placed immediately next to it, holding the racket in a left-handed version of the eastern grip. There are admittedly a number of players who prefer to use the right hand in a semi-continental grip or even an eastern grip. But these are players who are particularly skilful at using their left hand, and such variations can only be re-commended in exceptional cases.

The ready position

The ready position before the execution of a stroke will naturally be different for almost every player. It will depend on a number of factors, such as the racket position, the stroke technique, and the standard and confidence of the player's forehand and backhand; it will even vary according to the height of the player and whether he

The typical starting position used by Boris Becker

prefers to play offensively or from the baseline.

The basic position is as follows: stand with your legs a shoulder-width apart and your knees slightly bent; put your weight on the balls of your feet and bend your body forwards slightly. Your weight should be evenly distributed between both legs, so that you can move as quickly as possible in any direction. Hold your elbows close to your body – as Boris demonstrates so beautifully in the picture – so that you can swing your arm back quickly and without hesitation.

The left hand is placed on the neck of the racket. The right hand usually holds the racket with a forehand grip. This way, the player can step across to avoid a backhand, hitting the ball with a forehand stroke; and it is often possible for a player to hit fast-approaching balls using a backhand stroke in combination with a forehand grip, thus creating underspin.

The head of the racket should not be much higher than the wrist, so that too much time is not lost as the arm is swung back. This is particularly important with topspin strokes, in which the arm has to be swung in an arc well below the level of the ball.

Where should you position yourself? If you are at the back, then you should stand about a metre behind the baseline. If you are at the front, you should be about three metres back from the net. The exact distances will of course also depend on your individual reaction time. The baseline starting position also depends on technique. Players

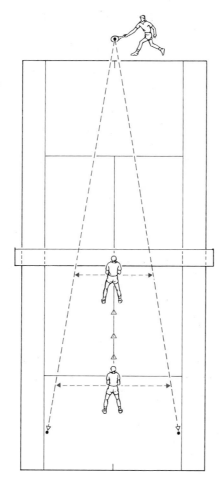

Playing from the net shortens the distance required to reach the ball

who prefer to use topspin will usually move slightly further back, because the extra movement which is needed for this stroke requires a little more time. The flight of the approaching ball will be a split second longer, thus allowing more time for the preparation and execution of the stroke.

The starting position by the net will of course depend on the height of the player and on how well he can control his shots. A tall player with a good, confident smash can come closer to the net, where it is also easier to play volleys. Moreover, the closer you are to the net, the smaller the area you have to cover in order to return the approaching ball (see illustration) – which effectively increases your reach both to the left and to the right. (For more about this, see **The return of serve** on page 44.)

Footwork

The footwork required of a tennis player is in many ways similar to that of a boxer. Both have to move fast and in small steps within a relatively small area, and both must be able to change direction very quickly. For a tennis player, good footwork forms the basis of a confident stroke technique. If you can move quickly into the hitting

A player uses ordinary running steps to cover longer distances

position, you will have more time to carry out the stroke – and the more time you have, the more confident you will be. Fast footwork also raises your chances of retrieving the ball in apparently hopeless situations.

Side-steps are used to return to the ready position, or when you only need to cover a short distance to reach the hitting position. *Cross-steps* are mostly used when moving into the hitting position or for making attacking shots. Ordinary *running steps* are most often used when you need to cover longer distances, either to get into a new hitting position, or when returning to the ready position.

Stationary shots
A stationary shot is when the player keeps both feet on the ground throughout the stroke. The same applies whether you adopt a sideways or an open stance in relation to the ball. You should always aim to bring the body into a sideways position, placing the front leg (left in the forehand, right in the backhand) forward of the point of contact. Immediately before ball contact you should transfer your weight onto the front leg. Don't forget what you are doing with your knees: the lower the ball comes, the more you have to bend them. Then straighten your legs again as you hit the ball. The more power-fully you straighten your legs, the more topspin you will get in the ball. Good tennis is not just a matter of using your arms but your legs too.

On clay courts especially, players very often slide into the hitting position. A casual observer might jump to the conclusion that they are hitting the ball during the slide. But this is very seldom the case with really good players, who usually stop sliding at the precise moment they hit the ball. The fact that they have returned to a firm standing position means they hit the ball with confidence.

Shots on the move
Hitting the ball while still on the move is an emergency measure when there is insufficient time to reach a standing position first. The basic rule is to make sure that at the moment of contact with the ball only the back foot is on the ground, and that the front foot doesn't come down until after this point. This technique is especially useful for forehand shots, though you should make sure that you turn your upper body sufficiently in the process. This combination of arm and leg technique is particularly to be recommended for attacking shots, since it allows you to run forwards towards the net in a single,

It is preferable to stand in a sideways position...

...But if there is not enough time for this, or you want to initiate an attack, you can always hit the ball while on the move

If you want to hit the ball at the best point, then mastery of jumping shots is essential

side of the court to the middle. Take off from the right foot with your body in open position as you prepare to hit the ball, and after ball contact land on the left foot.

Sometimes, in shots which require a lot of topspin, the legs are straightened so vigorously (see previous page) that at the moment of ball contact both feet are off the ground. Borg and Vilas both have perfect control of this stroke. In such cases of extreme topspin, one can land equally well on either foot.

Different strokes
Among world-class players, leg technique varies almost as much as stroke technique. Even when the same shots are employed, they use their legs in a totally different way. This is particularly obvious in the service and in the forehand. For example, the way Boris Becker crosses the baseline after his

uninterrupted movement. The automatic transfer of weight from the back leg to the front leg makes the shot more effective and gives it more power.

Jumping shots
As you would expect, a jumping

shot is one in which both feet are off the ground at the point of ball contact. This usually happens when the ball is very high and you need to jump to get the best hitting position. But you can also use a jumping shot when you want to move quickly from the forehand

service is by no means everyone's cup of tea. To do it requires not only a lot of take-off power, but also an incredible amount of coordination in the whole body throughout the manoeuvre, in order to make the whole thing run smoothly and in harmony. With Boris' vigorous service, you never have the impression that he could possibly be caught off balance.

For the "normal" player the classic procedure is more advisable: keep the left foot on the ground, and immediately after the shot step into the court with your right foot. This will not make you quite so famous as Boris Becker, of course, but at least you will avoid the frustrating experience of a series of double faults as you keep straying over the baseline!

Exactly the same applies to the topspin. Your shots will quickly lose their accuracy if you insist on hitting the ball with your legs in the air. Such a manoeuvre is particularly difficult with the forehand, in which you have to jump from your right foot to your left foot with your body in open position in order to make a jumping shot. You will need an incredible amount of ball sense and coordination if you want to make it look as elegant as Mats Wilander does. In such cases the moment of ball contact has to be absolutely precise; it is impossible to make any corrections once the body is in the air. Extra hip flexibility is also required, as it is difficult to turn the upper body when in open position. So keep your body safely on the ground – with one foot, at least.

The forehand

As has already been explained, the

forehand can be played with a variety of grips between the eastern and the western grip. If possible the ball should always be played with a certain amount of topspin. How much topspin there is depends on three factors: the grip, the position of the racket on ball contact, and the forward swing. The take-back will depend on the individual, but it must flow smoothly into the forward swing. The upper

body should be turned to the right. The stroke should consist basically of a forwards–upwards movement. Ball contact should take place in front of the left hip. The wrist should remain firm and the head of the racket should be vertical. The follow-through after ball contact is very important, but is far too often neglected. The racket should continue along the direction of the stroke and swing out towards the left shoulder.

Topspin is extremely important when playing the forehand

Forehand topspin

In the topspin stroke the flexing of the knees is much more important than in other strokes. This is because the player has to move the head of the racket sharply upwards and forwards from below. To achieve this the legs should be straightened so vigorously that it may even result in a jump. After ball contact the racket should be in *closed* position – that is, with the head facing downwards. This gives the player the feeling that he can't possibly hit the ball out.

There is no absolute rule for either the take-back or the follow-through. They can be modified according to the individual player, but should allow for a smooth, harmonious stroke. After ball contact the racket continues along the direction of the stroke, and the swing is supposed to finish high up near the left shoulder. Nowadays, however, one commonly notices that the head of the racket stops not at the shoulder but at the left elbow.

There is hardly a single world-class player who does not use a lot of topspin in the forehand. The one notable exception is John McEnroe. In my opinion, his forehand is not of the best; his grip prevents his stroke from producing much topspin. The best topspin control is achieved by Ivan Lendl, closely followed by Boris Becker together with three or four others. It is typical of all these players that they use a markedly eastern or western grip. This extreme position enables them to hit the ball a long way in front of the body. It also provides for more effective transfer of energy, and extra suppleness in the wrist before ball contact.

All this is as true for Steffi Graf as for Boris Becker. Their take-back does, however, differ in one or two details. Boris' elbow remains bent, and his wrist is in open position (with the back of the hand bent backwards). Because he doesn't straighten his arm, his take-back is correspondingly shorter, and the whole process takes up less time. This would normally result in the stroke losing much of its power, were it not for the marked flexing of his wrist.

Even on ball contact Boris' elbow remains bent and is held in towards the body – which is only possible because of his extreme forehand grip. The split seconds which are saved thanks to the smaller radius of the take-back and forward swing enable him to hit the ball more quickly. This also means that he can hit the ball very soon after it has bounced, which in turn enables him to supplement his power with that of his opponent. What is more, it allows Boris to shorten the trajectory of the ball, giving his opponent less time to prepare his next shot.

Such a technique, however, is not right for everyone. It requires an extraordinary amount of power in the lower arm and wrist. Boris has this – others haven't.

Steffi Graf, on the other hand, begins her take-back slightly later than Boris. This provides for better acceleration and timing. In exactly the same way as Boris, she tries to hit the ball as early as possible, thus enabling her to harness the energy which the ball has received from her opponent and add it to her own. Her forehand stroke is without doubt one of the best weapons possessed by any of today's top

women tennis players.

More needs to be said about footwork in the forehand. This stroke can be played either standing (whether sideways or open) or on the move or with a jump. Boris Becker prefers to play the forehand from a standing position. He holds his upper body sideways to the net for a very long time. Then just before hitting the ball he suddenly transfers his body weight and really launches himself into the shot. This is one of the reasons for the strength of his forehand. The same is true of Steffi's forehand.

Of course, very often a situation arises in which the player is forced to make this shot on the move or while jumping – techniques which both Steffi and Boris have fully mastered. At the sports centre we have coached thoroughly in all three types of leg technique for many years. Each player must decide which of them is the best to use in a particular situation. But these two players have trained for so long and from such an early age that the movements involved have become natural and instinctive, and almost take the form of automatic reactions to each situation. This is the only answer in the long run. If you have to think things over before hitting the ball, then by the time you have decided what to do, the ball has landed behind you!

Forehand slice

It is only for the sake of completeness that I have included the forehand slice at this point; it is of minimal significance in successful tennis. This is primarily because the forehand can be used with topspin in almost every situation, whereas this is not the case with the slice.

This stroke requires an eastern or a semi-continental grip, which is particularly suited to a low ball. The take-back starts considerably higher than with the normal stroke. The upper arm is slightly flexed, the elbow is held somewhat away from the body, and the racket is held in a slightly *open* position – that is, with the head facing upwards.

The stroke is executed with the arm straightened, using a forwards–downwards movement to produce the necessary underspin. In the slice, the wrist is held even more firmly at the point of contact, and the head of the racket is held vertical; only with a low ball can it be held slightly open. The follow-through again continues in the direction of the shot, though this time its path turns upwards as the racket is opened. With fast-approaching balls, the take-back and the forward stroke are markedly shortened – a technique known as the *chop*.

The backhand

In the backhand stroke the racket is held using the so-called continental grip. The player turns his body well to the left of the starting position. At the same time the left hand brings the racket well back into the take-back position. When the racket is furthest back, the right shoulder-blade should be pointing towards the net, while the right foot should be placed forward, pointing roughly in the direction of the left net post. The elbow is kept close to

The way Boris turns his body shows marvellous backhand technique

Leimen

There was nothing very special about Boris's name – according to his mother. In the summer of 1967, she had read a novel in which one of the main characters was called Boris. So in November, when her son was born, she told her husband that she wanted his name to be Boris. What could be more ordinary? There must have been thousands of babies who were named just like that.

Yet even Boris's name became a subject of interest in the summer of '85, when the little town of Leimen in Germany suddenly leapt into the limelight. A television commentator assured us that Boris was so named because his family had come over from Yugoslavia at the end of the war. One can only assume that the viewing public still believe that!

Leimen is nothing remarkable – a small town just outside Heidelberg with barely twenty thousand inhabitants. It has 108 clubs, of which 28 are sports clubs and one is a tennis club called *Blauweiss* or "Blue-and-White" The first recorded reference to Leimen is from 791 AD, when it was mentioned as a wine-growing area. But the parish did not achieve full town status until the early 1980s. The town boasts the remains of its ancient ramparts, and a 200-year-old castle in classical style, which is now used as the town hall. One of the town councillors who attends meetings there is an architect called Karl-Heinz Becker.

A few years ago the Baden Tennis Association decided to build a new sports complex in Leimen. It was to be a solid, businesslike structure – functional and in no way fancy. And the architect who was eventually given the contract was Karl-Heinz Becker, who played a little tennis himself. So it was quite natural that his son Boris should go along there to improve his strokes. "No," said Karl-Heinz, "we never pushed him into it..." "No", he said again later, when in the general euphoria that followed his son's victory his councillor colleagues pleaded for the young Wimbledon champion to be given the freedom of the town. As far as he was concerned, it was far too much for the lad.

Yes, everything was quite ordinary. That is, until the summer of 1985, since when many new-born baby boys have been given the name Boris, but this time not after the hero of a novel.

Left: The Becker family

Right: The Wimbledon champion receives a jubilant welcome in his home town of Leimen

The sequence of movements in the basic backhand drive

the body and is slightly flexed.
   Here too the take-back can be varied to suit the individual.

However, it shouldn't begin too high, because that will take up too much time. However good your backhand swing, it is of no use if the ball has gone past.
   The left hand should leave the

neck of the racket at the very moment the racket begins to swing forwards; but the hand should be left there for as long as possible, to ensure that the upper body remains balanced and that the body stays in a sideways position until the last moment. As the racket swings down, the body weight is transferred to the front foot (earlier than in the forehand). The arm should be straightened immediately before ball contact, which should take place in front of the right hip, somewhat further forward than in the forehand. The stroke itself should swing forwards and upwards. Even after ball contact, the upper body should remain in its extreme sideways position in relation to the net; this lengthens the hitting zone and makes the stroke more accurate. The racket performs a long follow-through in the direction of the stroke, giving the ball a small amount of topspin.

Backhand topspin
There is no important difference in principle between the forehand topspin and the backhand topspin. Both strokes involve an upwards–forwards movement and a

The backhand topspin is a very important stroke in modern tennis

pronounced straightening of the legs. Topspin specialists mostly use an extreme continental grip. The follow-through after ball contact often varies a lot; the arm

The backhand slice is mostly used in baseline rallies

can be straight or bent. Sometimes you can see how the player's upper body turns to the right with the force of the stroke; this of course means that the follow-through is significantly to the right.

Backhand slice

The backhand slice warrants considerably more attention than its forehand equivalent. It should be carried out using the continental grip, or in the case of low balls with the semi-continental grip.

The take-back in the backhand

slice goes higher than in the normal ground stroke; the racket is held slightly open, the upper arm is slightly flexed and the elbow is held away from the body. The arm is then straightened as the stroke swings forwards and downwards. The wrist is again held firm at the point of ball contact. It is absolutely essential to hit the ball well in front of the hip. At the moment of ball contact the head of the racket is again vertical; only with low balls can it be held slightly open. Players need to be continually reminded of this fact, because the average player tends to think that the racket should be held well open in the slice, and is then surprised to see the ball sailing in a wide arc over the court fence.

The follow-through again continues in the direction of the stroke, and only at this point is the racket opened. With very fast balls, both the take-back and the forward swing are very much shortened, because there is no time to do otherwise. This technique is known as the *chop*, and can often be observed in tournaments when someone makes a fast return.

Many taller world-class players – Victor Pecci or Yannik Noah, for example – employ this technique in particular against topspin specialists. This is because the chop allows them to give a very quick reply to the topspin, which is otherwise difficult to counter. What is more, the chop keeps the ball very low, making it extremely difficult for the topspin specialist to get his racket properly under the ball, which is essential for the execution of this spectacular shot. Really good players will have mastered all these variants of the

backhand, and will be able to swap easily from one to another – the fruit of good training. So you must practise them continually.

This is just what Steffi and Boris do – though I think Steffi could do with using her backhand topspin a little more often. Boris of course has a considerable advantage with his strong wrists, because it means he can change the direction of the ball at the very last moment, thus confusing his opponent.

The volley

Forehand volley

The most useful grip for the

forehand volley is a not too extreme version of the eastern grip. A lot of players make things more comfortable for themselves by using a semi-continental grip, because this can also be used for the backhand volley. A uniform grip can also be useful for dealing with low balls, when the racket is held slightly open. You don't have to change your grip, and so you save time. And you don't usually have much time when you're by the net, which is where nearly all volleys are played. The semi-continental grip

The volley is one of the most useful weapons in modern tennis

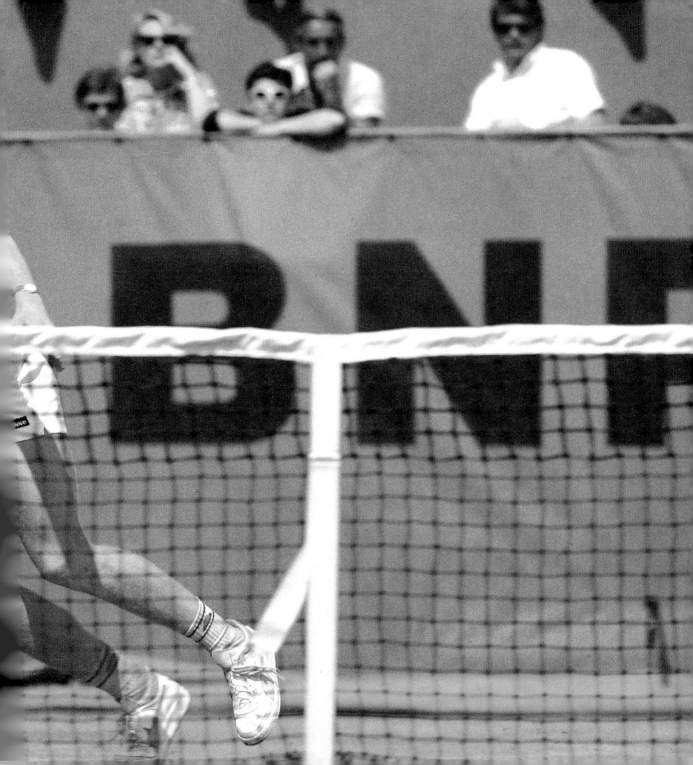

does not, however, allow for such effective transfer of power, and ball contact cannot take place so far forward.

The take-back is very short: the upper body is turned to the right,

The forehand volley

the elbow is bent, and the racket is raised and slightly opened. The racket is then swung forwards and downwards, and the elbow is straightened immediately before ball contact, which must be well in front of the body. Make sure that the wrist is held very firm. The

racket head should be vertical, and only opened in the case of low balls. This will give the ball the desired underspin.

The left foot doesn't come down until after ball contact. This enables you to put your whole body weight into the stroke, thus making up for

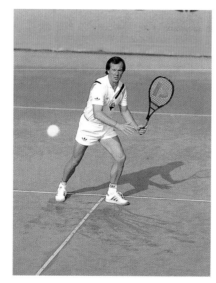

the short take-back, which otherwise militates against a hard shot. The follow-through is only short, and goes forwards and downwards; it mustn't be long if you are to be ready in time for the

The backhand volley

next shot. The follow-through must of course turn slightly upwards in the case of a low ball. Thus the ball will be given more underspin, while the left foot will hit the ground before ball contact. Obviously, if the ball arrives more slowly, then the take-back can afford to be more

generous and controlled.

Backhand volley
In principle the backhand volley is played using the continental grip. The only other possibility is the semi-continental grip, especially with low balls. The backhand volley

stroke is similar to the backhand chop (see page 31).

In the take-back, the upper body is turned a long way to the left, the upper arm is raised, and the elbow is bent and held somewhat away from the body. Here too, the take-back has to be very short; but the left hand should still hold the neck of the racket to keep it stable. The racket is held open, and should swing vigorously forwards and downwards to give the ball underspin. The left hand should leave the racket at the very moment it begins to swing forward, and should remain at the back to provide better balance; the right leg should move forwards.

The elbow is straightened during the forward swing. Ball contact should take place somewhat further forward than with the backhand ground stroke. The wrist must again remain firm during ball contact. The head of the racket should be vertical; only with low balls should it be slightly open. In the normal backhand volley, the right foot should not come down until after ball contact – though with low balls this happens before ball contact. Given the speed of the stroke, the take-back can obviously only be very short; with low balls the racket should be brought slightly higher.

As for the forehand volley, when the ball is approaching more slowly, giving you more time to prepare, you can afford a longer take-back and follow-through.

With both types of volley I have emphasised the underspin which the stroke gives to the ball. However, when the ball

An impressive display of high volley technique

An example to follow

by German Federal President Richard von Weizsäcker

At the age of 17 I was present at the 1937 Wimbledon Men's Singles Final, not as a player but as a spectator. One of the finalists that year was a quite outstanding German player called Gottfried von Cramm. He lost, unfortunately – but though we had so wanted him to win, we were able to accept his defeat. For he had brought honour to his country at a sad and difficult time.

Today we live at a time when our country is much respected by other nations. But this respect means that people like Boris have a responsibility, not only to achieve excellence, but also to conduct themselves well. It's a question of national pride, but not in the sense of putting other nations down. Rather, we should rejoice when a young man like Boris achieves such an outstanding performance and conducts himself so well at the same time. I am immensely glad that a German has won Wimbledon. But I am even more glad that he has done so with such good sense and decorum, and has thus set an example for young people.

We can think of all the coaches who devote weeks, months, even years of their unpaid time and effort towards training and encouraging the next generation of players – and at the cost of so much frustration. But now Boris has set a wonderful example of openness, good behaviour and determination to win that will inspire and motivate many thousands of young players to greater achievement, and their teachers and coaches too.

The champion talks to the West German President

approaches slowly it is also possible to produce topspin, though the technique is not simple. It requires a longer take-back, which is bound to take up more time, though it is still shorter than in the topspin ground stroke. But mostly you won't have time, and controlled ball contact will be even more difficult.

To be a good volley player you *must* have a strong wrist and powerful forearm muscles. Without these prerequisites a fast volley is scarcely possible – and fast it must be; for if your opponent manages to get to it, you will be too far forward to do anything sensible against a passing shot. Boris Becker fulfils all the physical requirements; add to that his technique, which he has practised till he can do it in his sleep, and of course his outstandingly fast reactions – and the result is there to be seen in tournaments throughout the world: a punishing volley which hardly gives his opponent a chance.

The service

Strange to say, every tennis player is aware of the importance of the service, but there are very few who practise it sufficiently. They probably think they're going to win it anyway, no matter what they do. And when they complain that they have "lost" their service, it soon becomes clear that they never had one in the first place! Every beginner will quickly realise that you can practically never be beaten provided that you always keep your service – in theory, not even in the

A Boris Becker speciality – service with an unusually high jump

The only tennis stroke over which your opponent has no control – if you always hold your service you can never lose the match

tie-break. There is only one piece of advice that I can give: practise, practise and practise again! A player who wants to turn his service into a really reliable weapon should practise about 300 services a day – there's no other way.

The only stroke over which the

Becker's service is said to be one of the best and fastest in the world, as this sequence of pictures clearly demonstrates

opponent has no control, the service should be carried out using the continental or semi-continental grip. In this case it is particularly

important for the tip of the little finger just to reach the end of the handle. This provides for greater freedom in the wrist, increases the

leverage and produces higher acceleration.

The game cannot start until you do, so take your time and choose your starting position very carefully. I personally would advise a position about 1½ metres from the centre mark. The feet should be a shoulder-width apart, with the left foot pointing up towards the right net post and the right foot parallel to the baseline. The complete stroke, which lasts no more than a split second, sounds rather complicated when explained in full. But if you ✴ read the description a second time, you will notice that it consists of four different movements which should run smoothly into one another to form a single harmonious whole.

The left hand will be holding one or perhaps two balls, and in the starting position it normally rests on the strings. But it is better in my opinion if the left hand grasps the neck of the racket as well as the ball. This helps the right hand to relax, which is very important.

The take-back begins with a pendulum movement in which the racket is brought back. It is important to execute this movement without any tension or expenditure of energy. At the same time the ball is thrown into the air from the outstretched left hand though it would be better to think of the ball as being pushed into position. The upper body is turned to the right as the weight of the body is transferred to the right foot; the knees are bent simultaneously.

The ball leaves the hand at about head height, and is pushed into the position where it is shortly to be hit by the racket – or perhaps a shade higher. Now the weight is transferred to the left foot as the pelvis is thrust forward. The upper body is bent backwards, combining with the legs to form a curve.

No later than the moment when the upper arm is parallel to the ground, the right arm is bent back. The head of the racket now describes a loop. At the same point the player straightens his knees, his upper body, his arm; and finally the wrist springs back, while the upper body is turned towards the direction of the shot. The racket hits the ball at the highest possible point, as it reaches its greatest acceleration.

So that the follow-through can also be incorporated smoothly into the whole movement, the left arm is simultaneously brought down into the pit of the stomach, thus allowing the racket to follow through past the left side of the body. Finally, the body follows the ball in the direction of the shot.

Apart from the ordinary service, players often use the variants known as the *slice service* and the *twist service*. In the slice service

The force of Boris's service effectively drives him in towards the net

sidespin predominates, while the twist service involves topspin. The slice service is produced by swinging the racket at a sideways angle from left to right, while in the twist service it is more of an upwards angle.

The slice service is produced by turning the upper body more sharply, whereas in the twist service the legs and body form a more clearly pronounced curve. Also, the first part of the follow-through is turned more to the right in the twist service than in the slice. In order to give the ball more spin, it can be placed further to the right in the slice, and further

to the left in the twist and not so far forward. But one should always try to place the ball in the same way, no matter which kind of service is used. This prevents the opponent from working out what to expect.

There is no doubt that Boris Becker possesses a quite outstanding service – perhaps even the best in the world. The type and direction of his service can only be recognised by his opponent very late, if at all. He always tries to vary the strength of the shot, and the spin and direction of the ball. This causes the opponent to hesitate and then make mistakes. The way his whole body is coordinated throughout the service is quite extraordinary. One is particularly struck by how much he

bends his knees and then flexes his body. He also bends his arm back very early.

All this together ensures the maximum possible distance from the lowest point of the loop to the point of ball contact, which in turn produces maximum acceleration. Further support is provided by the enormously strong wrist action when he hits the ball.

Boris' footwork is also worth mentioning. Immediately before ball contact he pushes himself off from both feet, hits the ball with his feet in the air, and lands on his right foot inside the baseline. Thus he has already begun the rush for the net, using the force of the shot to throw himself into the court. This jump has two advantages: firstly, he can hit the ball higher; and secondly, the scissor action of his legs in the air provides an additional impetus.

But for anyone who wants to imitate this service, I should add a word of caution: the Becker service isn't for everyone. He has the remarkable gift of being able to maintain 100-per-cent coordination throughout the whole manoeuvre from take-back to follow-through. If it is wrong in even the smallest detail, the whole effect is ruined – and the ball lands anywhere.

The return of serve

If there is a stroke which is generally practised even less than the service – although it is at least as important – then it is the return. And yet the movements and footwork involved in this stroke are completely different from all the other strokes – and, what is more, reaction training is essential for perfecting the return.

The starting position for the return has to be geared to the opponent's service. There is a simple rule for this: the harder the opponent serves, the further back you must go from the service line, and the shorter the take-back. For the second service, which is usually not so fast, you should move forward correspondingly. Another important factor is the particular technique which you intend to employ against your opponent's service. If you wish, for example, to reply with a topspin stroke, you must bear in mind that you will need more time for this than for a chop, so you will have to move further back still. This is even more true of the backhand topspin, as the whole process takes even longer.

The footwork in the return usually involves no more than one or two sideways steps, generally when the service is a fast one. You should step in towards the approaching ball. This makes the ball easier to reach and shortens its trajectory, giving the opponent less time to prepare the next shot. This is particularly important if you know that your opponent likes to move in towards the net when he serves.

It is of course best if you can play the return from a sideways standing position, but usually you don't have time for that. You are often forced to return while on the move, or even to play a forehand return from an uncomfortable open position.

When the ball comes straight towards you, you should make a

The return of serve with a short take-back is generally practised far too little

Above: The return often has to be carried out on the move

Below: In the smash the non-racket arm should point towards the ball

quick adjustment step sideways. But at the same time bear in mind that the take-back has to be shorter than with the normal ground stroke. The overall length of the stroke must therefore always be geared to the speed of the service.

Another tip for the backhand return, which so many players find difficult: when you take up the ready position, turn your racket and your upper body a shade to the left; the path of the racket is just that little bit longer than on the forehand.

Anyone who saw Boris Becker playing at the 1985 Wimbledon Championships will be fully aware of the quality of his return. More than once he was placed in that decisive situation of having to break his opponent's service in order to avoid a defeat. At such points he was helped, not only by his strokes, but also by his quick reactions and his ability to anticipate what his opponent was about to do.

The power in his wrist and lower arm enables him to get away with a short take-back and still come up with a fast return. Steffi Graf also possesses strong powers of reaction and anticipation, with the result that she was by far the youngest to join the exclusive "club" of the world's ten best players.

The smash

In the smash, the racket is held in the continental or semi-continental grip. The overall pattern of this stroke is in many ways similar to that of the service, but the differences are important.

The pendulum movement is omitted simply for lack of time; the racket is brought upwards and backwards across the right-hand side of the body. The upper body is turned less sharply than for the service. The left arm is outstretched and points towards the approaching ball; this provides some visual assistance and at the same time helps to lower the right side of the body, thus relaxing it a little. Again for lack of time, the looping movement is less pronounced than in the service – and finally the follow-through is shorter, finishing in front of the left side of the body.

The jump smash

Basketball can be a particularly good way of improving the smash

To reach the ball after the opponent has played a good lob, you are often forced to move backwards or to hit a jumping shot. You should move back in side-steps or cross-steps. In the jump, you should push off from your right foot, pointing upwards and forwards with your left to help balance, and land on the left foot following ball contact. While in the air, your legs should make a scissor movement. If the lob is deep, then the body may be forced to lean a long way back. The legs then make a more pronounced scissor movement, and the whole of the forward swing relies exclusively on the arm. This technique will clearly indicate the extent to which you have your body under control – a

matter of coordination. How much this is often lacking can be seen at any tennis club, where players will go out of their way to avoid playing this very difficult shot.

As I have said before, not everybody is a Boris Becker or a Steffi Graf. These two have refined their coordination to such a degree that every movement runs smoothly into the next and looks really easy. Boris understands every element of the jump required to create the optimum speed at the point where the racket hits the ball. What is even more amazing, he still finds the time to note exactly where his opponent is at any time.

The basketball training which we use at the sports centre is in my opinion a really excellent method of practice, especially for the smash. It helps you to train body coordination during the jump while at the same time making continual split-second surveys of what is happening. Eventually the whole thing becomes such a matter of course that no one can tell the amount of work that has actually gone into it.

The backhand smash

The backhand smash is without doubt technically the most difficult stroke in the whole game of tennis. Yet it is hardly ever given special consideration in the training programme – a great mistake. This stroke is usually executed while jumping. It requires a lot of strength in the wrist and lower arm, and also needs more body coordination than any other stroke.

The technique is as follows. The racket is grasped in the continental or semi-continental grip and

brought back over the left shoulder. The upper body is turned a long way to the left; the arm is raised so high that the elbow points upwards. As the racket comes down over the shoulder, the left hand supports the

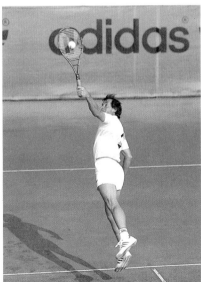

stance. The player usually lands on his left foot – although he may sometimes be able to perform a scissor movement while his legs are in the air so as to land on the right foot.

The backhand smash is certainly one of Boris Becker's most spectacular strokes; he almost seems to have been made for it. The reasons for this lie again in his extraordinary ability to control his body in even the most difficult situations, making coordination seem like child's play. Thus even in the most critical situations, he is able to run with his back to the net, jump up and hit the ball perfectly. His powerful wrist enables him to hit a really fast ball, and even to change the direction of the ball at the very last moment.

The lob

At one time the lob had a rather unfortunate reputation as the method used by women tennis players if they wanted to get out of a difficult situation. However, it has long since become a perfectly respectable technique, with its own place in the repertoire of any top-class player.

In principle there are two kinds of lob: the offensive or attacking lob, and the defensive lob. An attacking lob will send the ball flying over your opponent's head, allowing you either to score immediately, or else to drive your opponent into such a defensive position that you are able to take up the more favourable position by the net. An attacking lob should be hit as low as possible, and in such a way that the

neck of the racket, and the left shoulder is lowered. The player jumps up from the left foot, and immediately stretches vigorously upwards to hit the ball at the greatest possible height.

A vigorous flick of the wrist ensures that the head of the racket is turned forwards at the point of ball contact; after that the racket head is tipped downwards, while the body maintains its sideways opponent can't quite reach the ball. The ball from a low lob follows a shorter trajectory than a high one, leaving the opponent with hardly any time to get into position for a smash.

A lob is particularly effective if it sends the ball to the backhand side of the opponent's court. The opponent is then forced to reply with the notoriously difficult backhand smash.

The attacking lob is an especially good ploy against opponents who tend to come in too close to the net.

The lob is more than just a way out of awkward situations

Hair colour

Boris Becker was the first 17-year-old, the first German and the first unseeded player to become Wimbledon champion. And when a tennis player hits the headlines in the way that Boris did in the second half of 1985, then the media will scrabble for every conceivable snippet of news. Where *is* this little town of Leimen? Who taught him to play so well? What are his family called? When they asked him after that first Wimbledon final what he was going to do with all the prize money, he replied by asking them how much it was! And when they told him, his reaction was simply "What a lot of money!"

However, one of the hottest issues to be raised was nothing less than the colour of Boris's hair. You might question the relevance of the hair colour of a teenage tennis player, but that would be to misunderstand the ways of the media. There will always be a point when they run out of adjectives to use, and then they are compelled to resort to hair colour.

He was first described simply as "fair-haired" or "blond". But that wasn't felt to be enough, so someone then referred to him as a "flaxen-haired youth". Another called him "ash-blond", while yet another described him as "red-blond" – and one person even thought of him as "red-haired"!

The unbiassed reader, who has not seen Boris in the flesh, is left to imagine some compromise colour that combines all these elements. It is impossible to say whether the resulting conclusion is the correct one. You may of course argue that a tennis player's service is far more important than the colour of his hair; but you must admit Boris possesses a quite unusual head of hair!

The matter, alas, did not end there. The American magazine *Newsweek* found a completely new variant, describing the hair of this "German wunderkind" as "carrot-red". This must undoubtedly have influenced *Sports Illustrated*, the world's most popular sports magazine, which then turned from vegetables to fruit, concluding that Boris's hair was "strawberry-blond". You may be able to think of yet further possibilities. Or you might simply ask to look at Boris's passport!

By the time they have seen a few balls go sailing over their heads, they will stop going quite so close to the net, which in turn will make it easier to catch them out with a passing shot.

The defensive lob can be recommended for situations in which nothing else is possible – when the position seems hopeless and a passing shot is quite out of the question. The defensive lob gives you time and a breathing space. It allows you to get back into the middle of the court if you have previously been driven back to the edge.

The lob can also be very usefully employed when both competitors are playing from the baseline. A casually placed lob can knock the opponent out of his rhythm. You should, however, remember to give the ball as much topspin as possible, so that the player on the other side of the net is forced to reply from a long way back.

Now to the stroke technique: the lob can be played straight, with slice or with topspin. These days it is almost always used with topspin, especially when an attacking lob is intended. The movements involved differ only in detail from the basic forehand drive. However, the knees should be more bent, and the whole stroke should be started from a lower position. Also, in the straight or the sliced lob, the racket should be in the extreme open position on ball contact. The follow-through is considerably higher and more pronounced than that of the ordinary stroke.

Boris Becker's attacking lob with topspin is particularly worth noting; he does it so subtly that his opponent often doesn't realise what he is up to until it is too late to do anything about it. Boris also has a very good sense of when to hit a passing shot and when to hit a lob – which soon makes his opponent cautious when playing near the net.

The dropshot

In the dropshot, underspin is used to send the ball on its way. It is usually hit from between the baseline and the service line. It should be as low as possible, and should bounce very close to the net, forcing the opponent to run a long way to reach the ball. The dropshot is particularly effective when hit in the opposite direction from that in which the opponent is moving, thus catching him on the wrong foot. However, the important thing with the dropshot is to disguise it so that the opponent fails to recognise it at first; otherwise, being a slow shot, it will give him time to get to the net and be ready for it.

In world-class tennis, the dropshot is used far more by women than by men. One reason for this is that men usually play a more powerful game, leaving little opportunity for a dropshot to be used. Men also tend to play faster, and most of them are particularly good at playing near the net. However, if an opponent resorts to playing from the baseline, or is visibly off form, then men too will regularly employ the dropshot.

The drop volley

Of considerably more significance

The dropshot requires a high degree of ball sense

is the drop volley. A player can often be seen to make a fast ball almost drop from the racket by carefully relaxing his wrist. The ball then follows an unexpectedly short path and hardly bounces at all, so

that even the fastest opponent will have difficulty getting to it. The most appropriate time to use a drop volley is when the ball is hit very low. But even here, extremely sensitive racket handling is needed if the shot is to succeed.

The drop volley is technically very similar to the ordinary volley, though the whole stroke is performed rather more slowly. The racket arm should be slightly bent on ball contact, to make it easier for the wrist and lower arm to gently cushion the force of the ball. The follow-through is naturally very short, and when the ball approaches very fast there is no take-back at all.

Some players who are known for their unusually good ball sense use a backhand drop volley. The racket is held very open, and the path of the stroke and follow-through goes forwards and upwards. It is very difficult to foresee this kind of dropshot, and the strong underspin created makes it almost impossible to catch up with the ball.

Boris Becker has practised this shot for years, and has achieved almost perfect mastery of it. But in matches he hardly ever makes use of it as it is always an extremely risky technique.

The half volley

The half volley is when the ball is hit immediately after it has bounced. This situation occurs most frequently in the area of the service line. But a half volley can also be necessary in other parts of the court – for example, if you are forced to return the ball very quickly. The nearer you are to the net, the more careful you have to be with this shot. There is also very little time available to prepare for a half volley, making it difficult to hit the ball correctly. If there is still a choice between a volley and a half volley, choose the volley every time: it's much safer.

The half volley can be hit straight or with topspin. The decisive factor here is the angle of the racket. There is a logical rule for this: the nearer you are to the net, the more open the racket must be. The grip and the stroke pattern are similar to those of the baseline strokes. However, the knees should be more bent; the take-back is obviously considerably shorter; the forward swing is lower; ball contact takes place much further forward; and the follow-through is decidedly shorter, giving more time to prepare for the next shot.

This shot is indispensable in many situations, but its training is sadly very often neglected, even

The half volley is generally a rather difficult and risky stroke

though it has the additional advantage of improving ball sense.

The important thing with the half volley is to hit the ball well in front of you

The double-handed backhand

For decades you could count on one hand the number of well-known players who used the double-handed backhand. But now the situation has changed completely. A large number of world-class players have used the technique to great success, with

The double-handed backhand – a stroke with definite pros and cons

the result that others have imitated them. Children in particular have taken it up, since it is so much more comfortable for them. Their lack of strength has often created problems with the backhand, and the double-handed backhand has brought them quicker success.

But it is important to realise that the technique has both advantages and disadvantages. The advantages are the much greater energy transfer and the fact that the stroke can be better disguised to prevent the opponent from recognising it at first. Its drawbacks lie in the fact that the player cannot reach nearly so far and that his arm movements are considerably restricted. The last of these factors is particularly noticeable in difficult situations – for example, when the player is forced to play a shot from a wide position out of court.

There is no alternative but for the player to train specifically for these situations, so that he is able to use the single-handed backhand successfully as well. But a number of difficulties remain. Playing double-handed backhands from the baseline, while at the same time playing single-handed backhand volleys from the net, is bound to create problems, because the player will not be so familiar with the movements required.

The coach is invariably faced with some very difficult decisions. Should he limit his pupil to single-handed strokes? Should he leave him to carry on double-handed? Or should he wait until his pupil has grown sufficiently before getting him to change over to the single-handed backhand? It is best not to make such decisions until the coach knows his pupil extremely well. Knowing all his pupil's strengths and weaknesses, he can then weigh them up against each other: what will he gain? and what will he lose?

The most important requirements for the double-handed backhand are above-average speed (on account of the restricted reach), dexterity, quick reactions and anticipation. The double-handed backhand is played almost exclusively with topspin.

The right hand holds the racket in the continental grip, while the left hand is placed next to it in the eastern grip. Another possibility is for both hands to use the eastern grip.

There are a number of important differences between the double-handed backhand and its single-handed counterpart. The take-back is lower and the right arm is straightened. The upper body is turned during the forward swing so that ball contact occurs further forward, giving greater acceleration. The follow-through continues double-handed in the direction of the stroke and finishes at the right shoulder. Many players, however, can be seen to let go of the racket with the left hand following ball contact, thus finishing the follow-through single-handed. This has the advantage of keeping the body much better balanced in difficult shots.

Surprise shots

Every player will at some stage produce a shot that takes everyone

One of the ways to deceive the opponent – a surprise shot using wrist action

by surprise; neither the spectators nor the opponent could have predicted it. But a top-class player will deliberately add that element of surprise to even the most ordinary of strokes. For example, he might disguise the direction of the shot by changing the angle of the racket immediately before ball contact, or else he might pretend to be about to use one kind of stroke and then use another. The effect is particularly dramatic if the opponent is caught on the wrong foot. In top-class tennis such tricks are often important, indeed decisive, to

the game. After all, what is the use of the finest stroke technique if the opponent already knows what you are about to do with the ball? He'll be ready in position before the ball is even over the net, and then send it whizzing back past your ear.

One example of a surprise shot is the one regularly employed by all the better proponents of the double-handed backhand. It enables the player to determine the direction of the shot immediately before ball contact, thus giving the opponent less time to prepare his reply. John McEnroe's service is another particularly good example of surprise. His extreme sideways position deprives the opponent of even the slightest inkling of where the ball might eventually go.

Boris Becker is similarly a specialist in the art of surprise. He has a number of natural advantages in this area: his enormous tactical ability, which is geared towards deceiving his opponent; his unusually well-developed peripheral vision; his ability to improvise; his creative imagination – and finally, yet again, his strong wrist, which allows him to delay the decision as to the direction of the ball until the very last moment.

Boris's peripheral vision is really extraordinary. However carefully he is watching the ball, he always knows exactly how his opponent is moving, where he is standing and how his weight is distributed.

There are of course situations in which it is impossible to see the opponent, even out of the corner of one's eye. At such times his imagination comes into play. He is

A successful dive and roll is no fluke. It has to be practised systematically – first on a mat and then on the court

able to imagine himself in his opponent's position – "What would I do if I were in his shoes?" I myself have been caught out by him many times, simply because I did exactly what he thought I would do. In order to develop an imaginative game, it is vital to broaden the training programme to include ball sports other than tennis. *Monotony is the enemy of creativity.*

Finally, there is that strong wrist of his, which allows him to speed up or slow down a stroke, so that he can make the final decisive adjustments at the very moment before ball contact. The body also moves deceptively, thus confusing the opponent even more.

The most spectacular of the surprise strokes is probably the one a player has to use when he has caught up with the ball but is forced to return it with his back to the net. What he then does is basically against all the rules: he hits the ball either over his left shoulder or between his legs or from the right side of his body. In the last of these three, ball contact must be a long way back, and the racket position must be carefully adjusted accordingly. What is more, it is essential to watch the ball closely – which is by no means easy in such a hard-pressed situation. But the player who brings this trick off can be sure of loud applause from the spectators.

Another surprise technique is the dive and roll which Boris Becker has made so popular. At the sports centre we have always taught the dive together with the roll, without which it wouldn't work.

There are a number of reasons for including the technique. First, it

enables you to save an otherwise hopeless shot, when the opponent is already convinced he has scored. Secondly, it can shatter your opponent's confidence, as he is forced to reckon with the fact that you can reach further than he would ever have thought possible. Thirdly, if the ploy is successful, it will boost your own confidence and ensure the sympathy of the public.

This dive-and-roll technique is certainly not everyone's cup of tea. But I still recommend all players to practise it. For even if you never consider using it in a match, it has a remarkably beneficial effect on body coordination. You should always practise it on a mat at first, so as to avoid any danger of injury.

Which strokes for which players?

Teaching good stroke technique is

no longer a problem for the tennis coach. It is possible nowadays, by means of videos and illustrated books, to break down each technique into its individual components and then to combine them together again. Besides this, a great deal of relevant knowledge is now available from research in physics and biomechanics. Thus coaches these days are well equipped for anything that might come their way.

Much more of a problem for the coach is working out which strokes are right for a particular type of player. The strokes must fit the player exactly, and so the coach must take time really getting to know the player. For example, a fully-grown player will be completely different from a child both in his strength and in the way he swings the racket. But the problem is concerned with more than just external physical attributes.

The psychological factors must also be considered: the player's temperament, how competitive or how patient he is, and how he channels his aggression. You can't make a baseline player out of someone who rushes to the net after every shot, and vice versa. These two types of player need to develop a totally different repertoire of strokes.

A player with a lot of strength in his wrist and forearm is able to get away with a shorter take-back. He can bring his racket forward more quickly, and hit the ball more accurately. He also finds it much easier to achieve ball contact a long way from his body. These are all factors which in modern tennis really sort out the wheat from the chaff. For a player who can hit a really fast ball goes into every match with an incalculable advantage.

A coach must pay particularly close attention when teaching children. They are not yet very strong, and have to make up for this by using a long, high take-back. But there comes a point – and the coach must be able to recognise it – when the player can begin to reduce the height and length of his take-back.

When Boris and Steffi first came to me, both of them similarly used a long, high take-back to produce the momentum needed to send the ball on its way. We reduced it in stages as they grew up – and successfully, too. In Boris's case this meant matching his stroke technique, and his whole way of playing, to his legs, which at the time were relatively slow. For him we chose strokes with less topspin, but which nonetheless produced a really fast ball, thus allowing him to score faster. But Boris was a sturdy young lad, while Steffi, on the other

hand, was delicate. With her it was a question of advancing in much smaller steps. It was lucky that her father was a tennis coach too, and together we came to the conclusion that we would have to go very carefully with her. We developed special exercises to strengthen her wrist and forearm muscles, which benefitted her considerably.

The service is yet another matter.

Steffi's best stroke is the forehand drive

For this a coach would normally expect a player to use a continental or semi-continental grip. But for children, or indeed for any beginner, such a grip is no good, as the wrist and forearm are too weak to hit the ball in this position. This means that a beginner has to start serving with a forehand grip, and then move gradually towards the semi-continental or continental grip. If the forearm and wrist muscles are steadily trained so as to become sufficiently strong and reliable, then the feel for the right

grip will develop naturally. This programme of gradual adjustment is far better for the player, who will also enjoy it more.

There are, however, not a few coaches who insist on their players – children included – moving from one grip to the other in a single enormous leap. In many cases this is quite impossible, because the player simply doesn't have the strength. But that isn't the only reason for not doing it this way: the sudden change will destroy the whole make-up of a player's

individual style, which is after all the first distinguishing mark of a really good player. I have a very low opinion of such stereotypes which stifle the individual personality. I would even go so far as to call them a nonsense. If every performer plays the same forehand stroke, then their opponents need only adjust to it once to achieve enormous success. It is as if they were always playing against the same opponent.

Every player should develop the style which suits him best in the light of his own physical and psychological make-up. You cannot expect to change an aggressive player who loves to take risks into someone who feels most comfortable at the baseline. The coach must be like a tailor making a suit, taking careful measurements to fit the training and the technique to the individual player. There are an infinite number of ways of playing good tennis – and each person's way is a different one.

Even as children, Boris Becker and Steffi Graf played tennis in a way which cannot be found in any book – even this one! This became increasingly true of Boris in particular. I often watched him and considered carefully which of his movements were superfluous, which of them were acceptable, and which of them looked in need of improvement. A player can only be gently steered, never pushed, towards an effective personal style. Deciding what is right in such circumstances is never an easy matter.

In my opinion there are three important points to think about when making such decisions. Firstly, is the stroke sufficiently

A remarkable feature of Boris's forehand is the pronounced flexing of the elbow at the moment of ball contact

effective for the player to score enough points? Secondly, does he play the stroke confidently, without continually making mistakes? Thirdly, is the stroke economical, avoiding any superfluous expenditure of energy?

While evaluating these points one should bear in mind the age of the player and the amount of training involved. There is no sense in taking immediate and drastic steps to eliminate faults, as this usually causes other aspects of the game to suffer. If a player's strokes are effective, confident and economical, a coach should rather consider why that is the case, and whether it may in fact be possible for the technique to be used by other players of a similar make-up. In this way the coach is actually learning something from his pupil.

If you are thinking of changing your stroke technique, you should first consider carefully whether this is really worth doing. If you decide to go ahead, you should make the change outside the competition season. Otherwise, whenever it is vital to score, you will simply slip back into the old familiar habits. This is a matter which concerns the mind as much as the body (see **Training the mind** on page 81).

The development of talent

It is said that champions are born, not made – but this is not entirely true. Rather, champions are born *and* made. What this means is that greatness is not just something you are born with; you must work for it too. Talent isn't enough on its own; training is needed as well. There is no such thing as a champion who has achieved greatness on talent alone.

For a tennis coach, the discovery of a talented pupil is only the beginning of the story – the point at which the real work begins. Training children is scarcely comparable with training adults; both the content and the intensity of the training are entirely different. Variety is the watchword with children – never allowing boredom to rear its ugly head. Training sessions should never be too long, since children are unable to concentrate for long periods, and will constantly be in need of short breaks. But these breaks need not always be complete rest; they can be an opportunity to present the children with new tasks, or to report on previous tasks and analyse their results. The important thing with children is for them to enjoy what they are doing – in short, motivation!

It is a great mistake not to allow children to play anything other than tennis. This may well improve their game in the short term, but in the long run it will prove detrimental to their performance. Young players can only hope to reach the top of their game if their training programme is sufficiently varied to provide the greatest possible range of different movement patterns. Such training will later be of enormous benefit to their learning and tactical ability, and to other areas that are vital to good tennis.

Boris Becker is a model example of this, though it must also be pointed out that not only was he incredibly talented, but he was extremely lucky in other respects too. Living so close to the sports centre in Leimen, for example, was a great advantage, because of the expert guidance which was always on hand. His father Karl-Heinz, who is a good friend of mine, left his son's tennis education entirely in the hands of the Baden Tennis Association and those working in it. There were the

Stages in the development of a tennis champion

Association's youth officer, F. Adam, and sports officer Wolf-Dieter Späth, both of whom looked after him and guided him. They went to great trouble on his behalf, managing his career for him in consultation with me, right up to the time when he signed up with Ion Tiriac in spring 1984.

I coached Boris almost every day for nine years. Towards the end of that time, Erko Prull assisted me with physical training and Prof. Hans Steiner in the area of psychological training. I believe I was a fairly hard coach where Boris was concerned. His father never interfered, and usually took my side in any disagreements that occurred between Boris and myself. That needs to be said, because there are so many instances in sport of parents who take their children's side in everything, thus undermining the authority of the coach.

The consistency with which Boris was treated meant that he had to argue out every problem himself, and had no one to fight his battles for him. This helped him not only to develop his personality, but also to be decisive in matches, when a player has to make decisions quickly and for himself. I also think Boris was lucky in having the same coach for the whole of that period. It can be very bad for young people if they are always having to change coaches; each coach will have his own individual philosophy about training and match preparation. The players concerned will always be having to adapt to this, with the result that for a time their

Martina Navratilova and Boris Becker

development can be halted or even suffer a setback.

Another significant factor was a decision by the German Tennis Federation, on the initiative of R. Schönborn, chief coach in Heidelberg, to plan a programme of medical examinations as part of a research project in the field of sports medicine. A team of experts was appointed to carry out these examinations under the direction of Prof. H. Rieder, head of Heidelberg University's Sports Science Institute and one-time champion javelin-thrower. I was in this team, and was responsible for testing motor ability. The programme involved testing and analysing all the individual factors that together determine sporting performance. The results of the tests on my own pupils mostly corroborated what I already knew, but they provided a secure basis of scientific evidence. An effective training programme could then be planned for each player on the basis of individual strengths and weaknesses. The tests often revealed physical defects in young players, which meant that we could formulate specific exercises to compensate for each defect and hopefully eliminate the problem.

These tests were particularly important for players like Boris and Steffi, who had played tennis from a very early age. It was possible, by means of careful measurements, to predict how tall they would eventually grow. This in turn made it possible to work out the most appropriate techniques and strategies at a very early stage, knowing that they would be correct later on. For example, players who we knew would remain fairly short were encouraged to concentrate on the baseline game. Boris, on the other hand, was expected to grow to a height of 1.9 metres or about 6 feet 3 inches (he in fact grew to 1.91 metres). He was therefore able to concentrate on the serve-and-volley game which was to be so vital to him later on.

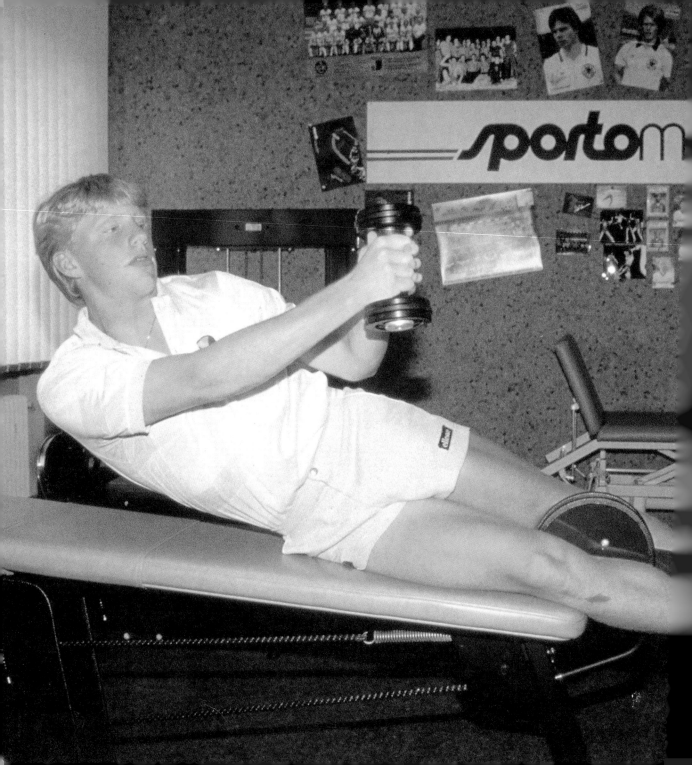

Training for competition

Take a young player who is known to have talent and to be well motivated. If his coach is good, he will have started to plan out his future with a lot of insight and understanding, and with the knowledge that he will continually have to make changes and amendments.

As young people grow up they are gradually able to cope with a greater physical load. The rest periods built into the programme become gradually less frequent; the training sessions increase in both duration and intensity. Because of the player's increased physical capacity, changes are also introduced into the content of the training; the varied programme which is so essential for children gradually gives way to a programme more specific to tennis.

The best form of training schedule is one which is divided into sessions. There might, for example, be two or three training sessions per day with recovery periods in between. The length of these sessions will of course depend on the age of the player and on the level of performance he has reached.

As regards the content of the training sessions, you should make sure that specific technical training, with all the corrections and adjustments involved, comes

before the rather more physically demanding conditioning training. This is quite simply because the fatigue resulting from conditioning training hinders the player from learning and performing the finer and more difficult techniques. Technical training should therefore come immediately after the usual warm-up session.

This should be followed by a series of exercises which concentrate on speed and muscular power; these should be of high intensity, and interspersed with proper rest periods. Finally comes a longer period of endurance training, in which the body is pushed to its performance limits; the various forms of tennis drill exercises are particularly suitable here.

It is not always possible to incorporate all three types of training in one session. But whatever types of training are included in the session, they should be planned in this order:
1. Exercises involving fine coordination.
2. Speed and muscular power.
3. General and muscular endurance – for example, match training, or games such as football, hockey and basketball.

(Compare Boris Becker's training programmes on pages 70 and 71.)

A dumb-bell exercise

A typical training week for Boris Becker during preparation for the 1982 outdoor season (outside school term)

Day and time	Content of training session	Intensity	Coordination required
Monday			
8.30-10.00	Slow running in steady state, interspersed with short loosening-up and stretching exercises	low	low
10.30-12.00	Improving technique (refining skills already achieved)	low	high
15.00-15.45	Flexibility exercises	low	low
16.00-17.30	Specific training for getting used to clay courts	medium	high
18.00-19.00	Football	medium-high	medium-high
Tuesday			
8.30-10.00	Long warm-up run/training to improve starting speed	low/high (short with long rests)	low/high
10.30-12.00	Improving technique	low	high
15.00-15.45	Stretching exercises	low	low
16.00-17.30	Specific training for getting used to clay courts	medium	high
18.00-19.00	Basketball	medium	medium-high
Wednesday			
8.30-10.00	Long warm-up run/arm and leg coordination	low/medium (short with long rests)	low/high
10.30-12.00	Broadening the technique repertoire	low-medium	high
15.00-15.45	Muscular endurance (circuit training)	medium	low
16.00-17.30	Training in the service and the return	medium-high	high
Thursday			
8.30-10.00	Fartlek training	low-medium	low
10.30-12.00	Service and return training (playing for points throughout)	low	high
15.00-15.45	Skipping exercises	low-medium	medium-high
16.00-17.30	Specific training in tactics	medium	high
18.00-19.00	Handball	medium	medium-high
Friday			
8.30-10.00	Long warm-up run/mini-games	low/medium	low/medium
10.30-12.00	Correcting individual weaknesses in technique	low-medium	high
15.00-15.45	Muscular endurance training using a medicine ball	medium	low
16.00-17.30	Match training	medium	high
18.00-19.00	Interval training on sand (12 x 200m intervals)	medium	low
Saturday			
8.30-10.00	Long warm-up run/training in take-off power	low/high (short, few repetitions, long rests)	low/medium
10.30-12.00	Tactical training with emphasis on defence and attack	medium-high	high
15.00-15.45	Coordination exercises	low	high
16.00-17.30	Match training	medium	high
18.00-19.00	Football	medium-high	
Sunday	Training-free day		

Specific forms of physical training

Coordination training

In the sports centre in Leimen, there has always been an emphasis on training to improve coordination. This consists primarily of exercises requiring careful coordination of the movements of the arms and legs. Limb coordination is essential if one is to play tennis well. Here are some examples:

● Sidesteps with arm circles forwards and backwards.
● Sidesteps with arm circles in opposing directions.

● Hopping forwards and backwards with various arm circles.
● Practising a smash without the ball and racket, while moving backwards into a straddle jump.
● Partner A stretches out his hands to touch Partner B gently on the palms of the hands. Partner A then starts to run in all directions

A typical training week for Boris Becker during the 1982 competition season (inside school term)

Day and time	Content of training session	Intensity	Coordination required
Monday			
15.00-15.30	Warm-up – loosening up – gentle stretching	low	low
15.30-17.30	Games designed to improve ball sense	low	medium-high
17.30-18.00	Gentle warm-down run	low	low
Tuesday			
14.30-15.00	Warm-up and stretching exercises	low	low
15.00-17.00	Correction of technical faults noticed during matches	medium	high
17.15-18.00	Hockey	medium-high	medium-high
Wednesday			
14.30-15.30	Warm-up/training to improve arm movement and starting speed	low/high (short with longer rests)	medium-high
15.30-17.15	Drill exercises/match training*	very high/high	high/high
17.15-18.00	Football	high	medium-high
Thursday			
15.00-15.30	Warm-up/compensatory exercises	low/low-medium	low
15.30-17.15	Match training	medium	medium-high
17.15-18.00	Basketball	medium	medium-high
Friday			
15.00-15.30	Warm-up using coordination exercises	low-medium	high
15.30-17.15	Service and return/match training	low/medium	high/high
17.30-18.00	Gentle warm-down run/gentle stretching	low	low
finally	Massage		
Saturday/Sunday	Tournaments		

* Wednesday matches were usually four sets; Boris often played two opponents because of his unusually strong game

(forwards, backwards, sideways) over one half of the tennis court. Partner B tries to move with Partner A so that Partner B's palms remain as much as possible in contact with Partner A's. The exercise can later be made more difficult by getting each partner to keep a distance of 30 centimetres between his hands and those of the other.

Skipping exercises
One item which has proved invaluable in improving coordination is the skipping rope. Steffi Graf hardly ever travels to tournaments without her skipping rope. Boris had a few problems with skipping at first, which he solved within a few weeks by taking a rope home with him and practising there until he could do it. Here are some exercises, some of

which have been devised by the players themselves:
● Running forwards while skipping, with one pass of the rope for each step.
● The same again, only backwards.
● The same again, with sidesteps.
● The same again, only the direction keeps changing as determined by the coach.
● Hopping forwards and backwards while skipping.

On the court
There are obviously many coordination exercises which can be carried out on the tennis court itself. Here are a few examples:
● The player takes up the sideways starting position at the baseline. A long, fast ball is played to a point behind him, which he has to return very fast, without being

allowed to take up a firm hitting position. This is a good way of practising arm and leg coordination.

● The player takes up a squatting position behind the net, and a low fast lob is played to him. He has to jump up from both feet, turn in the air and hit a smash.

● The player stands behind the net, and balls are played to the right and left of him which he can only reach with a dive and roll; he is supposed to roll as skilfully as possible. To avoid any danger of bruising or injury, mats should be laid out on the court for this exercise.

● Football with the tennis ball in the service court: the ball is allowed to bounce twice, and must be touched at least twice before it is played over the net.

These exercises can be made more difficult if higher levels of coordination and ball sense are demanded from the player.

Reaction training

It is a common misconception that quick reactions are inborn and that nothing much can be done to improve them. Even slow players can speed up their reaction time considerably with the appropriate training. Here are some suitable exercises for use on the tennis court:

● The player stands on the court and has to return a whole series of balls which the coach plays to him in very close succession. If required, the tempo can always be increased by shortening the distance between player and coach.

● The coach plays a series of smashes. The player stands immediately behind the service line and tries to return the balls.

● The coach serves from the service line and the player has to return every ball (an exercise I often used with Boris).

All these exercises involve hitting the ball as fast as possible so as to minimise the time the player has to react. There are a number of possible variations. Several players, for example, might be pitted against one player on the other side of the court.

Training ball sense

There are even ways of improving ball sense, which can be very enjoyable if properly organised. Here are some examples:

● Tennis in the service court, in which volleys are also allowed.

● The player has to play a backhand volley with so much slice that it enters the opponent's court but bounces back over the net. (You might offer a reward – a drink, perhaps!)

● Volleyball-tennis: the performers keep playing high volleys to each other from the service court, and try to catch each other out with dropshots and lobs.

Ranger training

This is the name given to a form of group training which is particularly good for increasing endurance and willpower:

● The coach stands on one side of the net, while the players form a queue on the other side. The coach plays shots which are geared to each player's particular level of skill. Each player in turn is given one or more tasks to fulfil (an attacking ball, advance to the net, volleys, smashes, etc.). When he has finished he must gather up his tennis balls as quickly as possible, return them to the coach and join the end of the queue. It is important

for the players to keep moving all the time, even when they are forming the queue or while the coach is correcting them. This exercise should last about ten minutes.

Stretching programmes

Conditioning programmes include various stretching exercises (see pages 73 and 74). They are divided into two main categories: dynamic stretching exercises and static stretching exercises. Thorough warm-up is essential beforehand, especially before embarking on dynamic stretching exercises (see page 95).

Strength programmes

In tennis the main physical load is sustained (in right-handed players) by the right side of the upper body. The game is played mostly with the body bent, which leads to a shortening of the flexor muscles and to relatively weak development of the buttock and rear thigh muscles. Weak stomach muscles will lead to the pelvis being wrongly positioned.

For this reason, it is important in tennis to do compensatory exercises to develop these weaker muscles as well. On pages 75 and 78 are some compensatory strength exercises which we have used a great deal at the sports centre in Leimen. They can again be divided into two categories: isometric exercises (static), and isokinetic exercises (carried out slowly and evenly against the resistance of a partner).

We train general muscular endurance mostly by means of circuit training (see page 78).

Dynamic stetching exercises

Funnel-shaped arm circles – forwards and backwards

Windmill-style arm circles – forwards, backwards, and in both directions simultaneously

Rhythmic leg swings – forwards and backwards

Bending the upper body sideways in a swinging motion

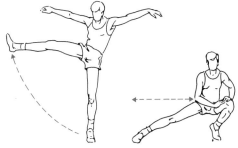

Swinging the legs – alternately sideways and in a figure of eight

From a crouch position, transfer body weight onto alternate legs

Backwards-turning knee-bends, moving the right hand towards the left heel and vice versa

Alternating quickly between stomach and hurdle positions

Alternating between the neck stand and a hurdle position with the body bent forwards

Alternating between round back and hollow back positions

Static stretching exercises

Tennis requires a high level of muscular power in the arms, especially in the service, for which we chiefly use the following two exercises:

● Two-arm throws using a medicine ball weighing one, two or three kilos (Boris used three kilos from the age of 14). This exercise is deliberately carried out using both hands, to avoid adding to the one-sidedness of the torso muscles.

● One-arm throws using a one-kilo sling ball, imitating the movements of the service.

In both these exercises Boris was always the best in his class; and of course his service has been the best in his class ever since!

Endurance training

For endurance training, we have always concentrated on *aerobic* endurance (with adequate oxygen). The opposite of this is *anaerobic* endurance (under oxygen debt), which is not generally applicable to tennis; besides, such forms of endurance training can hardly be expected of young players between 10 and 14.

We limit children under 14 to fully aerobic long-distance runs lasting between 30 and 45 minutes. After that age we introduce so-called *fartlek* runs (in which the tempo is varied) lasting about 30 minutes, and also interval runs (for example, 12 runs of 200 metres apiece).

Steffi is above average in terms of her endurance capacity, just as Boris is in the area of strength. Given the appropriate training, Steffi could have easily become an extremely good middle-distance runner. At the age of 15 she could achieve quite astonishing

Examples of strength exercises

Body roll until the hands touch the box

Raising and lowering the pelvis (isometric)

From the supine position, place the outstretched legs to the left and right alternately

From the prone position, raise left arm and right leg simultaneously, and vice versa

From the crouch position, raise left and right arm alternately

From hands-and-knees position, raise right leg...

...and left arm simultaneously, and vice versa

Raising the body from the side position with the legs held down

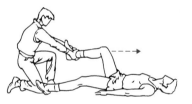

Knee raises against the resistance of a partner (isokinetic)

Raising the lower leg against the resistance of a partner (isokinetic)

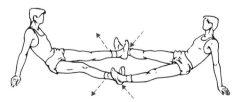

With feet astride, try to pull your legs together against the resistance of a partner (isokinetic)

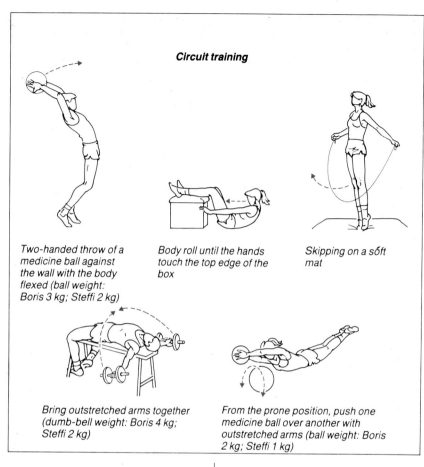

Circuit training

Two-handed throw of a medicine ball against the wall with the body flexed (ball weight: Boris 3 kg; Steffi 2 kg)

Body roll until the hands touch the top edge of the box

Skipping on a soft mat

Bring outstretched arms together (dumb-bell weight: Boris 4 kg; Steffi 2 kg)

From the prone position, push one medicine ball over another with outstretched arms (ball weight: Boris 2 kg; Steffi 1 kg)

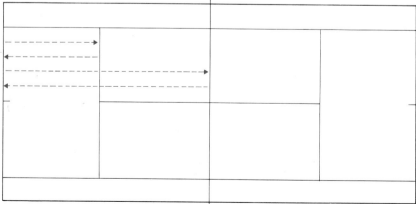

Short sprints are useful for improving speed endurance

performances over 3,000 metres. Hence she never had to concentrate very hard on the area of endurance training.

Short sprints are a good way to improve speed endurance (see diagram below left):
● The player sprints from the baseline to the service line, back to the baseline, and then to the net and back to the baseline again.

Steffi was 13 and Boris 14 at the stage when we doubled (or sometimes even tripled) the length of these exercises. We naturally incorporated suitable rest intervals between each sequence.

Another form of training which helps to improve speed endurance is an exercise using sidesteps to match the movements of a partner:
● Partner A moves in quick sidesteps to the left and right in a completely random sequence; Partner B stands opposite him, and tries to stay in the same position relative to Partner A by making the corresponding sidesteps. After 30 seconds of activity there is about a minute's rest, and then roles are reversed. Apart from endurance, this exercise also helps to improve agility and reaction time.

Young players have great fun doing one of our "Leimen Circuits" (see diagram below right), which improves coordination as well as speed endurance.

In an exercise to improve starting speed, players do a series of short sprints, using different starting positions for the sake of variety. They may start in an upright or a squatting position, or even lying on their stomachs. A set of these sprints consists of four or five repetitions, during which players loosen up as they trot back to the

Endurance training on a cycle ergometer

and players must not run while actually holding the frisbee. If the frisbee drops to the ground, then it is passed to the other side, who may also gain possession of the frisbee simply by intercepting it in flight. This game is useful for improving speed and reactions, and also for developing a good wrist action.

Lightning-ball
Two teams of four players apiece stand opposite each other. Each team must try to carry the ball over a touchline and touch it down. The ball doesn't have to bounce, so the game can be played on soft ground or sand. The ball can be thrown in any direction. If the player in possession of the ball is touched by a member of the opposite team, he has three seconds to throw it backwards to someone else in his team – otherwise he loses the ball. This game is very strenuous as there are hardly ever any pauses.

Special exercises for Steffi and Boris
In Steffi's case we had to concentrate especially on a set of

starting position. Each set is divided from the next by a rest of about four minutes.

Almost every conditioning training session is arranged to include a game of some sort – football, basketball, hockey or some mini-game. All team games will have at least some beneficial effect on the players' general fitness, and have the added advantage of developing good social relations between them. Boris used to prefer football and basketball, while Steffi preferred hockey.

Here are two examples of mini-games we have invented:

Ultimate Frisbee
Two teams of four players apiece stand opposite each other. Each team must try to get the frisbee over a previously-agreed line by throwing it forwards between them. The frisbee must always be caught,

An example of a "Leimen Circuit"

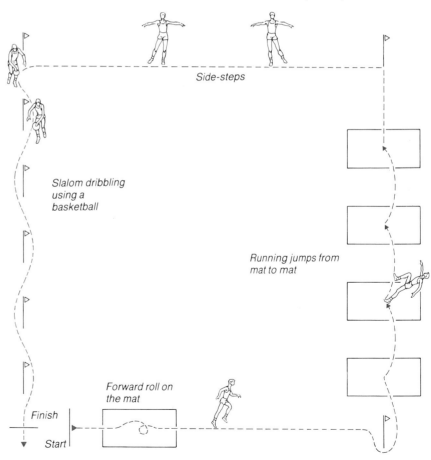

Side-steps

Slalom dribbling using a basketball

Running jumps from mat to mat

Forward roll on the mat

Finish

Start

79

specific stretching exercises. These were designed to compensate for muscle shortening in the areas of the back, pelvis and thighs (see diagram on page 81). The intensive use of these and other daily stretching routines over a period of two years ensured that she not only compensated for these weaknesses but achieved above-average flexibility in the muscle areas concerned.

The results of extensive observation and analysis indicated a need for her to do some work on her ankle and leg extensor muscles. She therefore included a set of step-ups in her training programme (see also page 81), which brought about a considerable improvement. Her enormous progress in this area became apparent in the jump-and-reach test (see also page 81). At 14 she could reach no further than 25 centimetres; but only 18 months

Leg-strengthening exercises on a weights machine

later she could manage an astonishing 45 centimetres.

Steffi's relatively weak ankle muscles necessitated yet another special form of training. She did skipping exercises on a soft mat, beginning with six sequences of 30 seconds apiece. When she was later tested she was once able to skip for two and a half minutes non-stop. If you're not impressed by this, just try it out for yourself!

In Boris' case we concentrated on developing endurance, having quickly realised that there was potential for improvement here. Boris's endurance programme between the ages of 13 and 15 consisted initially of long-distance runs at a relatively low speed (aerobic), leading eventually to shorter, more vigorous runs which brought him to the anaerobic threshold. These faster sessions were made up of two 3,000-metre runs with a ten-minute rest in between. At the age of 14, his pulse-rate at this speed was 180.

At our annual fortnight's training camp in Yugoslavia, we trained

Sideways skipping

players in deep sand on the beach using the particularly strenuous interval method. They first did six repetitions of 200 metres (in 45 seconds) with 90-second rests in between; then after five minutes' rest they repeated the same sequence again.

Boris hardly ever came top in this, but it was noticeable how he was always among the last to give up. How seriously he took his endurance training, and how much his ambition was goaded by his not being the best at it, is underlined by the fact that on his free weekends he would undertake extra endurance training. And because the tempo alone wasn't demanding enough, he would do it wearing a 10-kilo weighted vest.

Another vital area for improvement was his starting speed. We had to work to improve his coordination at the start, and to

Special exercises for Steffi Graf

Flexibility exercises:

Sitting in a tuck position, take hold of the soles of both feet, and stretch out each leg in the air alternately

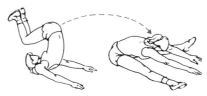

From a neck stand, lower your legs until they touch the floor well behind your head; bend your legs and roll forwards again until you are sitting with your legs apart, and bend your body well forwards

From a neck stand, move your legs and body in a circle to the left and to the right

Strength exercises:

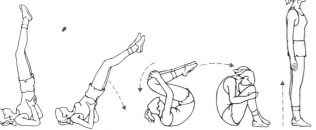

From a neck stand, roll forwards into a standing position without putting your hands on the floor

Fast step-ups, with or without weights

Jump-and-reach test

The Boris shuffle

make his steps quicker. Here are some exercises which we got him to concentrate on:

● Skipping on the spot, leading into a sprint. (It was probably skipping that gave birth to what was later known to Becker fans as the "Boris Shuffle").

● Running in quick steps against the resistance of a partner.

● Skipping uphill, up a 15-metre-long, 20-per-cent (or one-in-five) slope.

● Short runs up flights of steps – quickly, and stepping on every one.

Training the mind

The psychology of training and competition

Up to a certain point it is possible for any player to advance simply by mastering the techniques. But if he is going to develop further, and hopes eventually to get into major championships, then good tennis strokes will have to be matched by a high level of tactical ability, self-confidence and determination. And this is where a player's psychology begins to count towards his results.

Hardly any player need worry about such things as long as a match is going well. But when the match becomes critical, the winner

The importance of conviction

Steffi Graf has always relied heavily on strokes which she is absolutely sure of. This is of course perfectly correct in a match, but it did cause problems during her early training, when small adjustments often needed to be made. Her groundstroke swing, for example, had to be adapted as she grew older. At the age of ten she had to swing the racket a long way back to produce a hard enough shot. But by the time she was 15 she was strong enough to make do with a much shorter take-back, which takes up less time and makes for a faster game.

It always took ages to convince Steffi of the need for such changes. She held obstinately to any stroke which had given her success in the past. Sometimes it even ended in tears, simply because she refused to acknowledge that it was all in her best interests. Her father, Peter Graf, and her coach often had to spend days trying to convince her.

Not until she was fully convinced would she seriously apply herself to the task of learning the new technique. But when she did, she set about it with such enthusiasm that she was bound to succeed. This only goes to show that children cannot be forced into anything. They must always believe in what they are doing, and must be convinced that it has a useful purpose to fulfil.

Steffi always loved playing tennis, but this also meant that unlike some players she was reluctant to broaden her training with other games such as football or basketball. It wasn't that she was afraid of hurting herself in the rough and tumble; it was simply that she didn't enjoy them.

Then one day a game of indoor hockey was included in the programme. This time Steffi came along, grabbed a stick and joined in the game. The others looked on in astonishment as she stopped, dribbled and hit the ball as if she had practised the game for years. She immediately raced to the top on her performance evaluation for this part of her training.

In the meantime, Steffi has long since discovered the joys of basketball, and sometimes trains with the basketball squad at the sports centre in Heidelberg. She knows how good it is for improving her ball sense.

will be the one with the best-developed psychological armoury, who copes best with the stress.

These psychological abilities are in my opinion latent in every child. The differences only become apparent when the coach tries to awaken and tap this potential – a process which doesn't usually take place until adolescence.

Boris Becker showed the right attitude from the very beginning, and to an extent that I have never seen in any other player. Between the ages of eight and ten he was just as enthusiastic as the others, and played the game with the same inexhaustible enjoyment. But more than that, he very quickly revealed one of the important traits which was later to make him a Wimbledon champion: a total commitment towards summoning every ounce of strength in order to win or to shrug off defeat. Such willpower is to my mind absolutely vital at every stage of a match, no matter whether the player is winning easily or seems on the road to defeat.

It is all too easy for a coach to rejoice at a player's willpower but otherwise to continue as before. That is not a very helpful attitude. It is much better to consider ways in which this willpower can be strengthened yet further.

One vital factor is the behaviour of the coach himself, who must be ready to demonstrate his own willpower – not only in words, but in the unhesitating self-confidence he reveals in his actions and decisions. He will thus have a positive influence on the character development of the young player in his charge. The resulting behaviour traits will be difficult if not impossible to change in later years.

For the child always imitates the adults around him, identifying with those he wishes to model himself on. The process is not so much conscious and deliberate as instinctive and unnoticed. But it will influence the child in his day-to-day training, in situations requiring concentration and care, or when there are tasks to be carried out or weaknesses to be overcome.

There are many coaches who measure their success by how closely they have adhered to standard training methods and practices. This may appear quite satisfactory to the outside observer, but I doubt whether it will benefit the young players being coached. Neither will it, I believe, produce any really top performances. This can only happen if the player becomes aware of the coach's total commitment and is infected by his enthusiasm.

Another vital ingredient, apart from willpower, is the ability to concentrate, and this is particularly essential in tennis. The player must maintain concentration even when he is exhausted or in danger of losing the game. Concentration can then come to the aid of willpower, enabling him to mobilise and consolidate that last ounce of strength – perhaps just enough to tip the balance and turn the match in his favour again.

Finally, the player must have confidence in his own ability to perform, and this can only develop if he is certain that his performance has a sound and reliable technical basis. Technical stability can only be achieved very gradually, and it often takes a long time before it is sufficient to produce the kind of self-confidence which is so

manifest in the world's top players.

These factors are all interdependent: good, reliable technique induces self-confidence, and self-confidence aids willpower, which in turn aids concentration. How much of them a player has can be seen from his reaction to victory or defeat and the way he deals with them.

Willpower, concentration and self-confidence, therefore, are the foundation stones on which a future champion must build. In modern tennis, however, the development of these mental abilities requires more than just the instinctive understanding (if any) of the coach; amateur psychology is simply not enough. A coach needs to be able to work systematically in this as in other areas – in short, he needs proper psychological training.

There are two forms of psychological training, which in practice should complement one another:
● Systematic psychological training under the guidance of an expert, based on tried-and-tested exercises and procedures.
● Developing the right mental attitude towards situations, and communicating it to the player until it is imprinted on his subconscious.

One of the most noticeable traits of a fully mature champion is his outstanding ability to control and regulate the powers of which his body is capable, even down to the smallest detail. He must have the capacity to be fit and ready for action at exactly the right moment, to achieve full concentration, and to recover in the shortest possible time. The processes involved here are fairly complex, and depend for their success on methods of physical activation and relaxation that an untrained layman is rarely

Relaxation when changing ends

able to match by any conscious effort of will. If a top player is to defeat an opponent who is equally matched technically, then he must have that psychological edge.

This aspect of psychological training in sport is a question of attempting to influence the parasympathetic nervous system so that these capacities are improved. This is achieved by means of specific relaxation techniques. If such exercises are carried out regularly over a long period of time, they can eventually be used to considerable effect.

Relaxation exercises
Relaxation techniques fall into two categories: physical and mental. Both are important in sport, and can be used to improve performance.

Physical relaxation techniques
There are three kinds of physical technique which we use:

● Progressive muscular relaxation
● Yoga exercises
● Stretching

Progressive muscular relaxation can best be explained by describing the processes involved. The subject tenses up each individual part of the body in turn (hand, forearm, upper arm, etc.) for a short time. When released, the body part relaxes automatically, and the subject concentrates his attention on the sensations involved. The feeling of relaxation brings with it a sensation of peace and warmth, which gradually spreads through the whole organism as the process of tensing and relaxing is carried on step by step through every part of the body.

The main reason why progressive muscular relaxation has become so popular in high-performance sports is because it seeks to gain access to the mind via the body. Moreover, after only a short period of training, a player can practise it at home – even in bed – so it doesn't interrupt the normal training process.

In *yoga,* and in the *stretching exercises* which have been derived from it, each relaxation phase is preceded by a phase in which the muscles are stretched. The important thing again is to concentrate mentally on the relaxation phase.

Mental relaxation techniques
In mental techniques, relaxing sensations are absorbed via the senses and processed in the central nervous system so that the sense of relaxation permeates the whole organism.

The most popular mental relaxation technique is probably that of *autogenic training* – a procedure that has been taken over from the medical profession. This involves the continual repetition of words suggesting warmth and heaviness. During the course of the programme, these repeated suggestions gradually induce the corresponding sensations in the body, which are comparable with those produced in the physical techniques.

With the tennis players that we have trained, we have refrained from using suggestion, and have turned instead to music – a resource which everyone can use, and which seems particularly suited to young players. We ourselves have always found that players will naturally turn to music while preparing for a match. And world-class players have often been seen doing the same.

Even the Walkman has its uses

Boris Becker's Walkman is a typical example of this. He always plays lively, jazzy music on his machine before a match, which has an activating effect on his system during match preparation. He is "psyching himself up" into the right state of mind. Some other players prefer soft music, because they tend to be too highly aroused and need to be soothed. Playing music on the Walkman has the additional advantage of shutting out much of the player's surroundings without cutting him off entirely.

Another form of mental relaxation involves *deep breathing techniques*. These are particularly relevant to tennis for a number of different reasons:

● Breathing techniques can be used to lower the body's arousal level at specific moments where concentrated rest is required. This is most noticeable when a player breathes out deeply as he is about to serve.

● Breathing techniques can be consciously used and controlled, while at the same time initiating unconscious processes of arousal and relaxation in the body. This can be used in the development of a specific breathing programme.

● Improved breathing helps the whole body to function better, on a physical as well as on a psychological plane.

The basic mental training which the young player undergoes should involve learning at least one of the relaxation techniques, or else a combination of different methods that is specifically suited to him. Initial training will normally last between two and three weeks, and will consist of daily sessions of about ten minutes apiece. During

this period, the coach or sports psychologist should always be present to advise, to prevent any outside disturbances and to make any necessary corrections to the procedures. Errors cost time and are difficult to eradicate later.

With regard to Boris Becker, I have already mentioned how much he likes to use music to assist the relaxation process – though he is missing the point when he says he only does it because he enjoys listening to music. However, he also includes breathing exercises in his training programme, so that he can then use them in specific situations in matches. Apart from that, he is particularly interested in the techniques of mental rehearsal, which have been practised in some form or other by practically everyone who has trained at the sports centre in Leimen. In my opinion, mental rehearsal is the most important psychological tool in the tennis player's repertoire, and no world-class player should try to manage without it.

Mental rehearsal

Mental rehearsal involves a process of continually repeating a movement or technique in the imagination. The player rehearses the movement in his mind's eye as though he were watching it on a film. The strange thing about this is that it releases tiny nerve impulses in the muscles as though the movement were actually taking place – the so-called Carpenter effect. Thus the body is in the process of learning while it appears to be at rest. The more intensely the player imagines the "film" to be going on and involves himself in the situation, the more effective the

technique. The whole phenomenon may seem incredible, but it is easy to understand the principle.

There is no harm, if the opportunity presents itself, in using video for mental rehearsal. Note also that every mental rehearsal session should be preceded by relaxation exercises. This will enable the player to shut out any external distractions and concentrate entirely on the mental processes involved.

Mental rehearsal has a number of applications in sports training:

For learning specific techniques
Mental rehearsal can, for example, be used to improve the service. Boris Becker once went through a phase of never placing the ball high enough; he always hit it too low, and the awkward angle caused him to make a lot of mistakes. It also interfered with the loop movement, depriving the ball of much of its speed. So we got together and worked out an imaginary sequence made up of the correct movements. Once Boris had this clearly worked out in his mind, he was able to rehearse it during his mental training sessions at home. Thanks to this and some actual practice with the ball, he was quickly able to eradicate the error.

For learning complicated movement sequences
A player once had problems with a particular sequence of movements. So we asked him to write down carefully the different movements involved. He then had to imagine them to himself as vividly as possible, and rehearse them mentally every day. An example of such a sequence might be "service

– forwards to the net". It is important to keep rehearsing the whole sequence until it is anchored in the subconscious and no longer needs to be thought out consciously.

During match preparation
Mental rehearsal has a special part to play here, since every match requires mental preparation – adjusting psychologically to the particular circumstances of the tournament, to the environment, and to the match itself.

The player will usually have familiarised himself with local conditions until they are imprinted in his mind, and will have made a careful study of his opponent. This will activate him for the competition

Aggression means pulling out all the stops

and reduce any doubts and uncertainties to the minimum.

The opponent is naturally at the forefront of his mind. If he is well known, or if they have often played each other before, then there will be no problems. But if the opponent is unknown, then if possible he should be watched during an earlier match. The player should then rehearse the opponent's characteristic playing methods several times in his mind's eye, trying if possible to get right inside his opponent's mind.

Improving aggression
Aggression is part and parcel of any high-performance sport. But tennis requires a special kind of aggression. A player needs to pull out all the stops if he is to act quickly and decisively during the

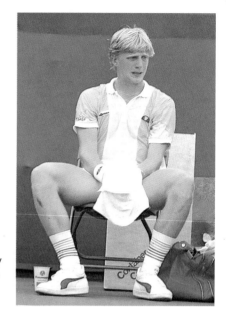

Ready for action

game, often driving himself to the very limits of his strength; but at the same time he should not let aggression take control over him, as this will only drive him to blind recklessness. A tennis player needs to be able to control his aggression with his mind and his intuition.

There are two areas of training which should include exercises for improving aggression: psychological training and training on the court.

Psychological training
The session should begin with relaxation exercises – music, deep breathing or physical techniques. This should then be followed by a period of mental rehearsal, in which the player conjures up unpleasant situations such as double faults, hostile jeering or unfair decisions

Self-confidence

There are plenty of tennis players who <u>dither</u> and <u>hesitate</u>. They are fairly easily recognisable, because as soon as they reach the critical stage of a match, a set, or even a game, they suddenly <u>forget</u> their <u>strokes</u>, or they <u>stop</u> hitting the ball and start <u>"pushing"</u> it. They seem primarily concerned with getting that round object over the net, no matter in what way, ignoring the possibility that the opponent may send it whizzing back past their ears. They will occasionally strike lucky if the opponent thinks in the same way they do.

This has a lot to do with self-confidence – the mark of a really good player. This is certainly true of Steffi and Boris, who sometimes give the impression that they would play a match point in the tie-break in the third set in exactly the same way as the first point in the first game of the match. They simply <u>get on with it</u>. This stroke has succeeded umpteen times before, so why on earth should it land in the net or go out this time?

Other players reveal their lack of confidence in different ways. They may, for example, decide that they will be quite happy to become 50th in the world ranking of players; and once they have achieved this goal, they may then consider the 20th place to be the highest that is worth striving for. Such players cannot be expected to achieve very much more. If you set your goals relatively low, you will admittedly suffer fewer disappointments and may feel more comfortable – though that is true of every profession. Not so Steffi Graf, who said at the age of 15 that she wanted to come first, not in Heidelberg but in the world. Perhaps there were a few who laughed at her then – but if so, they won't be laughing any more!

It is the same with Boris Becker. He was just 16 when he first came to Wimbledon in 1984. He had a look at the draw, and saw that he was drawn against John McEnroe in the third round. He sat down and thought about it, and after a pause he said, "If I beat McEnroe I'll be number 42 in the world!" He smiled as he said it, but underneath it all he was quite serious – yes, he really meant it! At the time he was well down in the 80s in the world ranking, while John McEnroe, whom he might actually be playing in the third round, was first in the world.

It was during this period that he appeared on the Centre Court one evening during a match between Ivan Lendl and the German Rolf Gehring. Boris sat down among the reporters in the press stand, while his coach sat further forward in the seats usually occupied by friends and relatives of players. "I want to see what Lendl can do", said Boris. Lendl clearly had the measure of Gehring. Boris watched Ivan Lendl closely for barely a quarter of an hour, allowing nothing else to distract him; you had the feeling that he was absorbing every movement that the Czech player made. Then he gave a deep breath and said to his coach, "Let's go, I've seen it all! He's really quite a good player!" The reporters laughed. This young "press assistant" might just as well have told them what a good writer Hemingway was!

The next day Boris was due to meet Bill Scanlon from Texas. At first he didn't look too well; he came to the side of the court and asked his friends, "Do you think I'd better shake hands with this chap here and now?" But he quickly snapped out of this – up to the point when he fell awkwardly, tearing two ankle ligaments in the process. That evening he was lying in bed in his hotel room, looking pale, and surrounded by a dozen or so tennis journals. The room became filled with more and more people asking how he was, and he replied, "Sorry you're so worried about me. It's not really my style to leave the court like that...!"

from the umpire. He should try to imagine them so vividly that his pulse rate increases. In the process he will learn to release exactly the right kind of aggressive feelings that are needed to cope with those unpleasant situations.

Aggression on the court
We have used a number of different games to improve aggression. Here is the method I used with Boris and Steffi. I would stand at the net and play the ball to them while they stood on the opposite baseline. They were not allowed to move backwards – only forwards – and they were supposed to return the ball fast so that it hit me. For every bull's eye they got a reward. At first it was no more than a fun exercise. But with time it became increasingly dangerous for me – and I had to move further and further back from the net.

We used to play a similar game in which they had to smash the ball; but I had to be careful not to make my lobs too easy for them. In order to increase their motivation still further, I would often swap places with my pupils for a short while. They would naturally use this as a means of measuring their skill against that of their coach.

Boris was always finding new ways of challenging me, and invariably made sure that his achievements were well rewarded. Simply by getting me to challenge him with apparently impossible tasks, he was able to relieve me of whole crates full of fizzy drinks! He eventually stopped using this method of getting drinks when he realised that training was sure to "earn" him a lot more.

Boris always sought competition in whatever form it took. It was always difficult to get him to do really hard training; he was then – and still is – a competitor of the most extreme kind. Other players would put far more effort into training but avoided competition; and as a result their match performance was way below what they could achieve during training. But Boris's attitude, and that of Steffi too, was completely the opposite.

Concentration training
Total concentration is one of the basic requirements for successful tennis. In those press conferences that normally follow a big final, there is hardly ever an occasion when the champion doesn't remark on how good his concentration was, and the loser doesn't complain about having lost his concentration. There are some players who can be distracted by the most trivial detail, and others who never lose their concentration until they are trailing behind – while others again refuse to be deflected by anything from their ultimate goal of success.

Concentration can be improved by the same means as aggression: psychological training and training on the court.

Psychological training
This again involves a preparatory relaxation session followed by mental rehearsal of specific techniques. But in this case the programme also includes external disturbances which imitate the atmosphere of a match. The player might, for example, run his imaginary film to the accompaniment of loud music on the car radio while sitting next to

the driver, or with his eyes open in front of the television.

Concentration on the court
The court offers a wide range of possibilities, the idea being to "sharpen up" some of the exercises you are already doing so that more concentration is required. The general principle here is that the faster and more difficult the task, the more effectively you will be able to "switch off" any external distractions and thus improve concentration.

Concentration exercises help especially in those difficult situations where you are in danger of losing concentration or have to get your concentration back. You might, for example, be suffering from exhaustion, or be about to lose vital points, a set or even the match. There are a number of approaches to this which in our experience have proved particularly effective:
● Learn to take account of nothing but the court and your opponent, and get your coach to keep drawing your attention to this point. You need to be able to shut out the whole of your surroundings, both visually and acoustically.
● Learn to switch over from one moment to the next. If it's your opponent's turn to act, then concentrate on his every move; if it's your turn to act, then turn your attention back onto yourself.
● Learn to make full use of the rests between games, especially when changing sides. You need to recharge the batteries as effectively as possible and renew concentration for the next game. You must first try to achieve a state of equilibrium: make yourself

Straightening the racket strings helps Boris to concentrate hard

comfortable, turn your attention inside yourself, and keep your movements and breathing calm. Develop your own ritual of unconscious habitual actions – actions that on the face of it are of little significance, but which give you a sense of familiarity and security. Boris Becker has developed the habit of always grabbing his towel in the same way, and always tapping his racket on his shoes in the same way. Before the game is resumed, you must get back into the right state of anticipation, arousal and concentration, no matter how the match is going. You need to learn to achieve this optimal state at exactly the right moment.

● Learn to watch the ball as intensely as possible. If you are hitting the ball yourself, the associated sensations should be so intense that it feels as though you are flying with the ball, or placing it in the opposite court by direct control. Only with this degree of concentration and imagination will you be able to achieve that feeling of being totally in control.

Playing with one ball
Concentration when playing on the court can sometimes be improved by the simplest of measures. You will naturally have a selection of balls for training purposes, maybe even a whole basketful. So when you hit a ball out, you probably take another one without giving it a second thought. And yet a useful exercise, both for concentration

and for avoiding mistakes, is to play for a short time with one ball only; when you hit it out, run over and fetch it back. You will thus become more aware of the mistakes you make – and you will inevitably concentrate harder on avoiding mistakes, simply to avoid having to run and pick up the ball.

Coping with stress
Tennis is a game where stress is unavoidable. If the player is to get used to the stress, then it has to be dealt with specifically in the training programme. Playing in a strong wind or serving against the sun can be used as forms of stress. When team mates play against each other, deliberate umpire errors can be introduced; or tournaments can be set up which lead to fatigue.

When Boris Becker's technique was sufficiently confident, I had to keep thinking of ways of making his training more rigorous and demanding. Once, for example, we went out in pouring rain onto a sodden court to play a set in impossible conditions. Or in bright sunshine we might stop changing sides so that he had to serve the whole time against the sun.

It goes without saying that the result of every tennis match is determined in its final stages. In the first game of the first match, it is easy to play well. The real test of a good player is his performance when it is five games all in the third set. We used to play through such situations again and again. I think Boris's incredible ability to pull off the "big one" at the decisive moment can be attributed to this particular form of training.

A born competitor

Ever since the time when Boris rose so meteorically to the top of his game in 1985, people have often asked me in what ways he was so different from other players. This is not an easy question to answer, even for someone who has worked with him for nine years. There are others who are equally good technically, and his footwork has never been his strong point; he can achieve an incredible level of concentration, but that is not enough on its own.

The real answer lies deep down in his nature; for Boris is a natural competitor: someone who hates losing and really loves to win; someone who never gives up, and who always strives to play better, even in unusual situations. It is possible to implant competitiveness and develop it in someone, but the result is never the same as with someone who is born with it. I can demonstrate this with a whole series of examples, which on their own might seem mundane, but which together provide a perfect illustration.

Once, when he was only eleven, he turned up for winter training with his nose all plastered up. He explained that he had been involved in a snowball fight. He had narrowly avoided being hit by one of these missiles at the very last moment; only he had somehow managed to impale his nose on a fence in the process! Others would have complained loudly at this, but Boris hailed it as a victory: "I must have reacted very well, because the snowball never hit me!" The fact that his quick reactions had caused him to cut his nose open was a purely incidental detail as far as Boris was concerned.

During his rise to fame, many others have noticed too how interested Boris was in all aspects of the game: how closely he watched his opponents and used these observations to work out the strategy for his next game against them; how he always decided before each tournament what his world ranking would be afterwards; and how he took note of absolutely everything to do with the game.

This reminds me of a particular final in the Baden under-14s championship, in which Boris played for the umpteenth time against his long-time rival Rainer Marzenell. Boris won the battle 7:5 in the third set. But the first thing he said was "Now at last I'm in the lead! I've won 13 matches to his 12!" No other player would have counted up all his victories and defeats against a particular player, let alone written it all down in a notebook. But this was natural for Boris. He never gave up until he won.

This trait of his showed up in other things that happened. Once, for example, the boys were larking about in an indoor court after training, and hit on the wonderful idea of throwing gym shoes at each other. They continued until a shoe somehow managed to get stuck on one of the beams in the roof. They began to throw balls at the shoe to try and "shoot it down". They did not of course meet with immediate success, and were soon interrupted by other players who had booked the court. They gave up the shoe for lost and left the court – all, that is, except Boris. Even the protests of the players who had just arrived were not enough to stop him going on, until at last he hit the shoe down, which he then held aloft like a victor's trophy.

He always sought competition, and more than that, he always had to win. I once took him to a golf course. Although he had never held a golf-club before, he could hit the little ball amazingly well after only a quarter of an hour, and immediately challenged me to a game. Another time, during a training camp in Portoroz, we were playing football on the beach.

Suddenly the ball fell in the sea. It was Easter, and the water was still unpleasantly cold. Almost everybody gave up the ball for lost, but not Boris. He dived into the sea and rescued it, because his team was losing, and the only way to retrieve the situation was to get the ball back.

Yet another example was in 1984 when, following an operation for the torn ligaments he had sustained at Wimbledon, he returned home to Leimen with his leg in plaster. But nothing could keep him away from the court. He was playing a game against our conditioning trainer, who is a very good amateur, when I arrived with a crowd of young players. I wanted to start punctually, but Boris protested loudly. He was losing, and he wasn't going to let himself be beaten by such a weak opponent, even with his leg in plaster.

Together these small episodes serve to underline the impression that we have of Boris – as a sportsman who enjoys competition, and seeks it out wherever he can. And as everyone now knows, he has certainly found it!

◀ *Typical Boris Becker*

In control of the situation ▶

The match

Preparation

Every match needs preparation, in tennis as in other sports, and not just at Wimbledon. This applies both to physical and to mental preparation. Many matches have already been won or lost before the first ball has been played.

Psychology

Mental preparations before a match should be modified to suit the individual player. The coach who has trained the player so far should by now have already given him plenty of useful psychological advice (see **Training the mind** on page 81). Apart from those specific mental preparations for the match, there are a number of everyday tasks which have a practical psychological significance. For organised planning is the bread and butter of life generally, whether in the job or at home – and tennis is no exception to this. Nothing should be left to chance.

For the player this means carefully assembling all the necessary items and equipment so that he has everything he could conceivably require; and this includes obtaining all the relevant documents and information. He must pre-empt every possible disturbance to the match routine. The player must pack not only his sports bag but also his psychological "bag of tricks", which means making a mental list of all the possible events which could conceivably disrupt the match. He should then be able to embark undisturbed on the immediate pre-match routine, which he should have long since practised and developed to suit his own individual needs (see **Relaxation exercises** on page 84).

But whatever a player's individual requirements, the pre-match routine must always put him in exactly the right frame of mind to give of his best. During the process of developing his game, he should have learned to judge his reactions to external circumstances and the appropriate ways of dealing with them. He should have become used to coping with problematic situations so that his performance is no longer affected. For example, if he has just arrived from overseas, then he may have jet lag to cope with; or maybe someone has just said the last thing he wants to hear at that moment; perhaps something has gone wrong with his equipment; or his opponent may be behaving in a way that annoys him. But nothing should be allowed to put him off his stroke.

Boris Becker's most spectacular stroke

Preparation involves more than just packing your kit

It is no use, however, just ignoring such disturbances or refusing to acknowledge them. The player must be able to accept their existence while remaining cool, calm and collected, and without letting them affect the mental state which he has built up. This is a skill which can be learned. There are some players who pick it up intuitively, while others have to be taught it systematically. Boris was lucky in this respect: even when he had removed the headphones of his Walkman, nothing could possibly disturb him.

Strategy
Irrespective of whether it is a club tournament or a Wimbledon championship, when he walks on the court every player should have

worked out a definite plan of action.

The details of this plan will of course depend very much on how the player judges his own capabilities. And as this is very difficult to do, it is important to have someone to consult well in advance. There is no sense, for example, in planning an offensive strategy if you simply don't have the technical ability required, or if your style of play is completely different, or if you are at your weakest when playing near the net. Equally, there is no sense in playing defensively if your legs won't move fast enough, especially if you have a fast shot to make up for it and a confident volley from the net. It would naturally be ideal to be a complete all-rounder who is good at absolutely everything – but no one can expect to manage that!

It is also important to be fully aware of the opponent's strengths

and weaknesses. Watching him in a previous match can be a good way of finding these out. Taking notes can be very useful here, and a few simple statistics can provide an incredible amount of information. It is certainly useful to have a coach or a well-informed friend to confide in; two pairs of eyes are always better than one. Coaches can also help by going round and "spying" on the opponent, in the way that football coaches do. In my opinion, far too little of this is done in tennis. There are players who keep a running record of all their likely future opponents and modify their tactics accordingly. René Lacoste of France was doing this back in the twenties, and Martina Navratilova got the members of her team to type this kind of information into a computer.

Boris Becker has always watched his opponents very closely – even as a boy, when he could only see them on television. I can still remember what he said when he became the youngest-ever German champion at the age of 15: "They can easily pick me for bigger championships. If I have to play against John, I've already planned the right strategy. I'll move into the net whenever I can, and get there well before him. This'll push him onto the defensive, and that's where he has one or two faults!" Boris wasn't joking; he believed it with all the earnestness of youth – and by the way, it was John McEnroe he was talking about!

You should never go into a match with the idea that it will somehow work out all right. You need to have a much clearer notion of exactly how best to tackle your opponent.

The knock-up before the match is your very last opportunity to make a few final observations.

Should you, for instance, use slice or topspin from the baseline? How do you know that? If your opponent likes to hold the racket in an extreme grip in a closed position, then slice is certainly the most appropriate tactic, because it is sure to give him problems returning low shots. However, if your opponent plays his forehand with a continental or semi-continental grip, then there is nothing better than using high topspin shots, even on the forehand. They will either force him almost to tear his arm off, or make him retreat so far behind the baseline that you have enough time to initiate your own attack.

On the other hand, if your opponent keeps scoring from the net and you have great difficulty in catching him out with passing shots, how about moving in towards the net yourself? – only faster than him! Then it will be a question of whether he has some good passing shots too.

It is also extremely important to have a fallback strategy up your sleeve. After all, it is always possible for your opponent to play you at your own game; your primary plans will then be of no avail, and without a fallback you will be at a loss. It is therefore important to be somewhat flexible. You should plan a definite strategy, but one which can be changed if necessary.

Such a situation can be due to factors other than your opponent. There may, for example, be external circumstances which force you to change your strategy.

Perhaps the wind gets stronger, or the sun starts to get in your eyes, or there is a change in temperature, or the ground is affected by changing weather conditions. You may even need to change to a racket with a different tension, which may mean switching tactics as well as technique.

Tennis is just the sort of game in which minor details can be enough to tip the scales between two equally matched players. So you need to have such details under control.

Warm-up

Every training session at our sports centre in Leimen is preceded by the same warm-up programme, which must be followed by every single player. It begins with a gentle ten-minute run, followed by a programme of stretching exercises.

Tactics

Singles

The tactics to be used during the match will depend firstly on the technical competence of the player himself, and secondly on that of the opponent. The external

Pre-match warm-up is vital for success

Pre-match stretching exercises

circumstances must also be taken into account.

Tactical ability
A player's ability to formulate and carry out a tactical move depends to a certain extent on his own native intelligence; however, this is not the "IQ" kind of intelligence. I have known players and coaches who were thought of as highly intelligent, but who seemed completely unable to act intelligently on court; it was easy to get the measure of them, and the intelligence which they used so effectively in their professional lives was of a kind that could not be applied to any practical situation in the game.

At the other end of the scale, there have been players who were not particularly intelligent in the way they dealt with life generally, but who revealed a very high level of practical intelligence on the tennis court and never ceased to surprise us with their achievements. And of course you find some who possess both kinds of intelligence, and others who have neither.

I would like to claim that Steffi and Boris are lucky enough to have both. Their general wit and intelligence has been obvious to television viewers in the interviews they have given – and of their practical intelligence in the game there can be no doubt. Their strategy is almost impossible to work out. On the other hand, they immediately notice their opponents' weaknesses and take full advantage of them throughout the game. They know exactly which shot they need to play in any particular situation to bring them success.

Percentage play

The kind of policy they adopt is commonly known as percentage play – an expression which first became popular in the forties and fifties when it was used by the American Jack Kramer. He knew, for example, that when he moved in towards the net, only 30 per cent of the passing shots against him would actually achieve their effect, and that the remaining 70 per cent already belonged to him. It was simply a question of planning his strategy on the basis of a cool and accurate assessment of what he had achieved during many years of training.

Baseline play

It is particularly important here to avoid the kinds of shots that are likely to produce faults. You only need to look at the records of past baseline games and you will come to some surprising conclusions. The player who wins is not the one who pulls off the spectacular stunt of just managing to scrape the ball over the net, but the one who keeps within the bounds of what he is sure of achieving. The number of faults which result from taking risks is always greater than the number of extra points that might conceivably be gained.

It is therefore better to keep your shots from going too low, and there is no need for every ball to land exactly on the line. You can even allow the ball to pass as much as a couple of metres above the net – in which case topspin is the appropriate technique, because it bends the trajectory of the ball so that it bounces earlier than expected. The same applies to a ball which bounces one, two or even three metres in front of your opponent's baseline. Here too, topspin can present him with problems, because the ball will bounce longer and higher and push him even further back.

The simplest solution

One of the typical features that marks out a champion is the way he always tries to score in the simplest way possible. For example, if your opponent is driven out of the court, leaving the whole of his court empty for you, then there is no sense at all in using some fancy shot to manoeuvre the ball over the net. An ordinary shot is quite sufficient – and this is what you will always see the world-class player doing.

Play decisively

Once you have decided to move in towards the net, whether after the service or after a good attacking shot, then you mustn't hang around in the middle somewhere, as this is the worst position you could possibly be in. Once you have made your decision, you must act accordingly. Use your imagination, and don't be afraid to take calculated risks.

The attack

If you move in towards the net, you must always remember to react more quickly, because the ball has less far to go. This means playing your attacking shot so that your opponent is in trouble and has difficulty in replying. You can put him in this position by using a fast and/or accurate shot, or by making a surprise attack; you might, for example, play a very long, high topspin shot, then wait till he has already returned it, or is about to do so, before moving forward.

On the other hand, if your opponent uses a very extreme grip on his backhand, and you are playing on a clay court that is damp and therefore "slow", then a long, low slice is undoubtedly a good attacking shot.

As to whether you should advance to the net after the service, this will depend on the quality of that service. One is always hearing players complain that they "haven't got a first service". I don't think much of such complaints, because if that were the case, I doubt whether they would have a second service either!

How regularly you advance to the net after the service will depend to a large extent on the type of court on which the game is being played. On the grass courts of Wimbledon it is impossible to imagine doing otherwise. A good player must never stay at the baseline after his service, but must always move forward. However, this doesn't mean charging blindly forward in the hope that you have hit a fast enough shot into your opponent's court.

The service

Even on a grass court, it is important to vary the service so that the opponent has no means of predicting how and where the ball will land – because as soon as he can do that, you have as good as lost the match already. If Kevin Curren could have guessed how and where the ball was about to be served in the 1985 Wimbledon finals, then Boris Becker would certainly not have become champion.

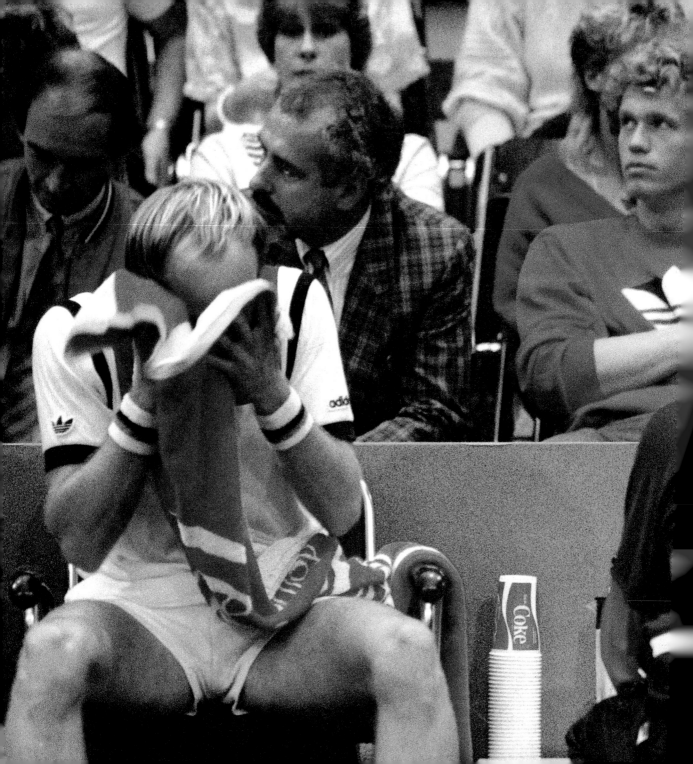

There is an infinite number of ways of varying the service – from the straight service which is aimed at the body, to the twist or slice service which drives the opponent out of the court. But whichever you choose, it is important not to make too many faults on the first service. In the Wimbledon final, Boris played 60 per cent of his first services successfully. That is good for a world-class player but by no means outstanding. You should always try to do at least as well; and never let yourself be lulled by the comfortable thought that there is always a second service to fall back on – because if you lose that second service, you won't have the chance of a third. So concentrate on getting it right first time! You will soon notice how much more successful you are. A double fault is a free gift to the opponent.

The return
The return is naturally much more difficult than the service, because you have to adapt to your opponent. You need to stand in the right position, and try to predict your opponent's intentions in order to prepare the right counter-action and to be in a position to carry it out. You must also consider the wind, the sun, the playing surface and all the other external factors.

If, having taken all these factors into account, you decide to position yourself as close to the service line as possible, then you will be hard pressed to find enough time to prepare a return which is not marred by faults.

If your opponent serves a very fast shot and immediately advances towards the net, then the best solution is to use a short take-back before striking the ball, so that it can hopefully be returned at his feet. You don't even have to return the ball very fast, but it is important to keep the shot low and fairly short. The opponent is then forced to reply with a low volley for which he is in an unfavourable position in relation to the net.

If in spite of a fast service your opponent stays back at the baseline, then you should play a long, high shot which gives you time to take up a new position in the middle of the court. But if the service is short and relatively weak, as is often the case with a second service, then it is time to move in to attack. Not only will you have a chance to score, but it will also worry your opponent. The mere thought that you may use his second service to initiate an attack will make him want to play his first service extra hard, producing even more faults. He will then attempt an even harder second service, which will frequently result in a double fault.

The defence
Attack isn't always the best policy. If you are playing against a good opponent, you will always find situations for which it is essential to have full mastery of the art of defence, especially when he is playing near the net. There are many ways of getting him away from there, but two strokes that I consider particularly effective are the passing shot with topspin, either down the line or cross-court, and the lob. A topspin lob is

particularly effective, since it may only be recognised very late, and the ball on bouncing almost accelerates towards the back of the court. Your opponent may be forced to look on helplessly as ball after ball sails past him, and will soon begin to wonder whether perhaps he ought not to move in so close to the net. But if he starts to hold back from the net, this is your best opportunity to try some passing shots.

It is important to hit passing shots as early as possible. This shortens the trajectory of the ball, leaving your opponent less time to take up a favourable position. You should always try to vary the speed and length of these shots, and to intersperse them with a lob or two. This will confuse your opponent, who won't know what to expect.

There will of course be times when the situation is quite hopeless, and a high lob is the only remaining solution. Don't hesitate to hit the ball as high as you can. It must come down somewhere, though preferably inside your opponent's baseline! The higher the ball goes, the more difficult it will be for your opponent to reply with a smash, and the more time you will have to take up a good position in the court.

Take your time
Take full advantage of the 30 seconds' rest that the rules allow you in between points. This is essential, not only when you have been running around a lot, but also when you have lost a point on a shot which seemed easy. You must be able to put it completely out of your mind and concentrate on the next one before continuing.

The same applies when you change ends. My advice is this: the worse the match is going, the longer you need to rest. Every second is vital, as it helps you regain your composure and concentration.

Doubles
Doubles play is often much faster and more entertaining for the public, which is one of the reasons why doubles tournaments have gained in popularity and importance in recent years. Doubles has its own set of big events. In grand slam tournaments the prize money for doubles has been considerably increased, and doubles has also become more important in the Davis Cup and in club matches.

With few exceptions, the most successful doubles pairs are those who have been together for a long time. A casual partnership has only a relatively small chance of winning any of the really big tournaments. Choosing the right doubles partner is therefore extremely important, remembering that two top-class tennis players are no guarantee of a top-class doubles pair.

The requirements for a good doubles player are a good service, a reliable return, well-controlled volleys and a confident smash – in short, the kind of play that is generally given the term *serve and volley.*

However, while two serve-and-volley specialists will often make a good team, this again is no foregone conclusion. They must also be suited to one another. For a start, one of them should prefer playing on the left and the other on the right. If one or other of them is forced to change sides, his

play will inevitably suffer. It is also
important for them to relate well to
each other on a personal level.
Each partner must be able to feel
that the other will stand up for him;
and each must know that if he
makes a mistake, the other one will
give him the encouragement he
needs instead of shouting him
down.

There are not many doubles
partnerships that fulfil all these
criteria – which means that a really
top-class doubles team should win
many tournaments.

Here are a few tactical tips for the
doubles game:

The best positions

Doubles players always make it
their aim to be first at the net.
Whoever gets there first is in a
position to take the initiative, and
the chances of winning the point
are very much greater from there. It
is vital to edge forward with every
stroke, and never to linger near the
service line. The opponents are
thus forced to hit low balls. These
are always liable to produce
mistakes, because if they are too
low they will land in the net.

The opponents' only other
defence is to hit lobs. But this is
where percentage play comes in.
For every lob that lands near the
baseline and cannot be retrieved,
there will be at least two or maybe
three lobs that can be countered
with a smash, which in most cases
wins you the point.

The doubles server stands
further from the centre mark than in
singles. The first service is even
more important in doubles than in

singles. This is because a weak second service will encourage the opponents to take the initiative and advance to the net. Another important tip is always to keep on the move. This improves your reaction time, and gives your opponents the feeling that you have the whole court covered.

The best position to be in is near the net, while the second-best is at the baseline; but the worst position of all is to have one partner near the net and the other at the baseline. Partners should therefore be careful to move forwards or backwards together, always keeping the same distance apart from each other. This has the effect of halving the area that each partner has to cover. The same applies when an opponent plays the ball to the side of the court; both partners must move towards the side in question, so that no gaps appear in the defence.

Play through the middle
You don't have to hit every ball towards the sidelines. It is really much more important to play through the middle of the court. If the opponent is standing at the baseline and the ball arrives near the centre mark, then it is very difficult for him to manage a passing shot because of the awkwardness of the angle. Volleys too, if played through the middle, are less risky for you and more awkward for your opponent.

Intercepting the ball
You should try to intercept the ball as often as you possibly can, "stealing" it from your opponent. Your partner must of course immediately cover the other side of

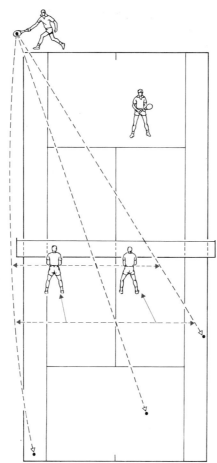

When balls are played to the side of the court, then both partners should move sideways as a team

the court. This will worry the opposition, who will tend to take more risks and make more mistakes as a result. If your partner is serving, then you will need to consult with him beforehand to prevent any gaps from appearing in your defence which might allow an opponent to score easily. If partners have played together for a

long time, then each will be able to sense what the other is about to do. And if that is already the case, then there is no doubt that the two are well matched as doubles players.

The tandem formation
A doubles pair is sometimes observed to stand in the tandem formation, otherwise known as the Australian formation. This is where the server and his partner stand one behind the other on the same side of the court. This formation is useful against opponents with a good cross-court return which keeps giving problems. The server must stand close to the centre mark so that he can move quickly into the empty side of the court. He should preferably serve through the centre of the court so as to avoid leaving his defences open. The opponent is forced to return with a down-the-line shot, which often produces faults. Or else he has to hit a cross-court lob, which has the disadvantage of a long flight time.

Psychological tactics
Successful tennis depends very much on a player's mastery of the psychological aspects of the game. One important factor is the need for self-confidence. How can you be expected to win a game if you start out with the idea that you haven't a chance? How are you supposed to win if a bad decision by the umpire puts you right off your stroke?

All really good players use psychology in their game, whether consciously or unconsciously. It sometimes involves no more than a few ploys which are transparent even to an outsider. But results show that even these can be effective. In such cases you have to

part of a player's normal way of behaving, without seeming contrived and artificial. Many players are thus able to arm themselves effectively for the most difficult situations. If you can take your opponent's very best shots without appearing to get ruffled, this is sure to impress. And if you can impress your opponent, then you have begun to influence his thinking.

There are of course players who need to create friction between themselves and others, whether it be the opponent, the umpire or the public. It helps them to produce the right kind of aggression. Or else they simply need to let off steam. We can all think of examples of such players who have stayed at the top of the world class for many years. But in spite of their success, I don't think much of their methods. With time, such outbursts will inevitably affect concentration, if only because they encourage hostility on the part of the spectators.

I can think of far more examples of players whose performance has been greatly enhanced by the certainty of public support, which inspires them with extra fire and determination. A player who has the spectators on his side has an incalculable advantage, and all that is needed to win them over is the right kind of attitude.

Tennis for older players

Everyone knows that the older a player is, the more difficult it is to achieve a good sporting performance. The body becomes less effective in a number of areas vital to performance, such as muscular power, endurance. reactions and flexibility.

But this is no reason at all for giving up the sport. There are other aspects of performance that are preserved or even improved. I am thinking especially of ball sense and tactical ability, both of which benefit from years of experience on the tennis court. If you can use these abilities properly, you will be able to play a convincing and often very successful game of tennis up to a considerable age.

You will need to make up for the weaknesses in some areas by working hard to develop your strong points. But there is no reason why increasing age should inevitably lead to diminished performance. Even if you have played little or no tennis before and have started as an adult, you will still be capable of better progress than you might expect.

Naturally, it won't just fall into your lap. You have to do that little bit extra if you find the going more difficult. It's not just a question of more training, a diet or extra warming-up; it can often come down to the equipment you use. It

is, for example, extremely important for an older player to make the correct choice of racket. I have even noticed that professionals change to a different kind of racket as they get older, preferring one which gives the ball more speed. You should choose a racket with fairly elastic strings at a tension of at least a kilo below normal. This will give the ball extra speed, and even with less power and a shorter take-back you will still be able to produce a hard enough shot. You will obviously need to check that the racket is also effective at slowing the ball down, as this is essential for good ball control.

The shorter take-back will also shorten the forward swing needed before ball contact; and this will enable you to hit the ball more accurately and further forward. This is especially advantageous with fast-approaching balls, as it makes up for your slower reactions and diminished anticipation of your opponent's intentions.

Tactics
You should pay particular attention to your tactics. You won't be able to move fast enough to try a serve-and-volley strategy, so it is important to make your opponent run around a lot more than you. This means hitting the ball fairly

Older players still have potential. Laci Legenstein was many times veteran world champion

111

early, which is made easier by the shorter take-back. It is not necessary in such cases to hit the ball very hard. It will be quite fast enough, thanks to the early ball contact and the extra speed given by the looser racket strings.

If you can play faster shots than your opponent, you won't have to move around so much, which means you will tire less quickly. If you interrupt the flow of the game with a few dropshots, making your opponent run after the ball, then you can be assured of gaining control of the match. You also need to make more use of the lob. Even if your opponent manages to reply with a smash, you should not let that worry you. The smash will use up more of his energy than any other shot in the game, especially if he has to jump for it. And you can be sure that as he tires he will be less inclined to attack.

Safety
The dangers for players in middle age are usually to be found in the players themselves. I am speaking here of the common tendency for older players to overestimate their powers. If you have played almost every day for ten years, and not too badly at that, then you will not be pleased to find that there are new limits which have to be observed. Sometimes the body itself protests when you overstep the mark, whether through pain or exhaustion. You should take note of such symptoms, and not try to get rid of them with medicine or supposed miracle cures.

It is very important to eat sensibly, though a strict diet is not absolutely essential. If you eat a large lunch with a few drinks as

well, and then go straight out onto a hot, sunny court, then you needn't be surprised if you don't feel too good!

Older players should pay particular attention to the care of the joint musculature. Stresses which the younger body can happily cope with are often too much for an older one. For this reason, warm-up is even more essential before every match,

At the 1983 Veteran World Championship – champion Istvan Gulyas (aged 52) and runner-up Laci Legenstein (aged 57)

however unimportant that match may be. A sensible and above all thorough warm-up routine is an absolute must before undertaking any sporting activity. It should last for as long as is necessary to get really warm, especially in the arms, legs and back. So every warm-up session should begin with a careful stretching routine. This should stretch the muscles, not overstretch them. You could use some of the exercises shown on page 74, though some modifications will be needed. Players who think they can do without these exercises will have no excuse as the problems and injuries mount up. If they are lucky, they will get away with a few strains, but if muscles get torn they may be forced to give up tennis for months on end.

We have already mentioned the need to be careful when choosing a racket. The same care and attention is needed when choosing other items of equipment too, particular shoes. It is essential to make sure that they fit properly and have decent soles that are well suited to all the different kinds of court. A sole that will not bend with the foot can cause serious strains. Soles should also be springy enough to prevent any jarring of the spine. Hard courts are not the only reason for this; older people, who are often overweight, tend to put more stress on the muscles, ligaments and bones as they move around.

Just as much care should be taken in other areas of clothing. On cool evenings, especially in spring, when you may not yet have got rid of the stiffness left over from the winter, you should always wear a sweater at the start of the game. Your shirt should always be sufficiently absorbent to soak up the sweat.

The need for caution is not over when the last ball has been played. What is the use of the best warm-up routine if you sit down in front of the club pavilion all bathed in sweat? That is simply asking to get sciatica! The shower is the place for everyone who has just played a match. And if you then feel an unpleasant twinge anywhere, there are soothing oils and creams which have a warming effect to help prevent further injury. But if possible, a massage is a better solution.

Provided you observe all these points, you will be able to enjoy playing tennis up to an age at which others would not even consider playing. And you needn't limit yourself to casual games at the club. There are veterans' tournaments these days, and also team championships for the various age bands, which are fought as hard and competitively as any professional tournament.

If you have continually lost against a particular opponent for as long as 30 years, then beating him at last in your mid fifties must be a wonderful experience. Victories in later life have their appeal.

The fitness which you need to continue playing tennis in your later years will also have a positive effect on your everyday life. You only have to think of Jean Borotra of France, who was the world's best player in the 1920s, and who even now in his eighties still looks on tennis as the elixir of life. Then there was the German player Gottfried von Cramm, who at 40 led the German Davis Cup team into the European finals in the early 1950s, and then became Germany's "Sportsman of the Year". Finally, there is the example of Kitty Godfree, former Wimbledon Ladies' Singles Champion, who is still playing tennis in her eighties.

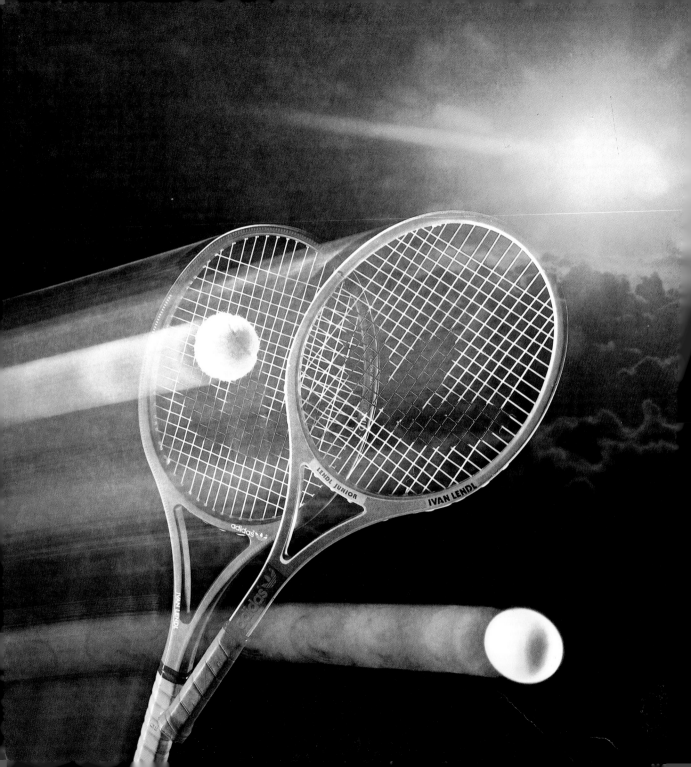

Equipment

The right equipment is essential for any sport, and particularly for tennis, where the choice of the racket alone is a science in itself. The outcome of a game depends to a surprising degree on whether the players have the right equipment, and there are too many players who don't realise this.

If you are not fully informed yourself, then it is vital to seek good advice about the correct choice of gear. If you go to an ordinary sports shop, you are unlikely to find anyone sufficiently knowledgeable about the construction and stringing of rackets to provide you with one that is exactly suited to your needs. Ideally the salesman should not only play tennis himself but also know how his customer plays. But that is unrealistic.

You will be doing well if you can find a specialist shop where you can get some advice from an expert (or, even better, hire a test racket). But even an expert will often find it difficult to work out what kind of a player you are. Some players will give a completely wrong impression of their standard and style of play, while for others it will be the first time they have bought tennis equipment.

So here are some general suggestions, which may be of help:

The correct equipment is a vital element of success

The racket

The important factors to consider when choosing a racket are the weight, the balance and the thickness of the handle, each of which needs to be matched to a player's individual requirements. When the racket is held correctly, the handle should normally be of such a thickness that the gap between the base of the thumb and the tip of the third finger measures the width of a finger. Too often, especially with small children, you notice that the handle is far too thick. There are two reasons for this: firstly, there are too few rackets around that are suitable for small children; and secondly, parents tend to give their children a somewhat larger size than they need on the basis that it will still be big enough for them in a couple of years' time. This is understandable, but it is not the proper way to learn tennis. A tennis racket is not like a garment that the child can be expected to "grow into"; it must "fit" the child straight away. Saving money is quite out of place here.

The mistake is further compounded if the racket is too heavy or too long for the player. The results are easy to predict: either the child will lose all interest in the game, or he will pick up a

The correct racket size depends on the age of the player.
From left to right: normal, junior and mini-rackets

dreadful technique, or he may even suffer actual physical damage.

So weight and balance are of equal importance when buying a racket. Beginners and/or children should have a racket which is fairly light and evenly balanced, which makes it much easier to hold. More advanced players will need to change to a heavier racket, but the correct choice will still depend on the player's physique and degree of technical skill. But by the time a player has reached this stage, there will most likely be a coach or a more experienced club member on hand to provide the necessary advice. A player who relies largely on technique, for example, should always go for a light racket.

Another important factor which varies considerably is the rigidity of the frame. A more rigid frame gives the ball more speed than a softer, more flexible one. But it also sets up much stronger and more unpleasant vibrations in the arm, especially if the ball is not hit in the exact centre of the racket. I would therefore only recommend a rigid frame for really good players who can hit the ball accurately.

If a player tends to suffer from tennis elbow, then he should definitely choose a more flexible frame which absorbs the vibrations set up in the racket. A racket with a large head can also be recommended, as it allows for a much larger "sweet spot" (or

hitting area) in the middle of the strings, considerably reducing the vibrations. This is the reason why these large-headed "fly swatters" have become so popular in recent years. Even many of the world-class players have joined this trend, because in their case the extra time lost due to injury means a considerable loss of income as well. Many others opt for the so-called mid-size racket.

The strings

When the racket hits the tennis ball, the two remain in contact for only four or five milliseconds. And yet many players claim – often rightly – that they are able to sense the differences in the ball and adjust the racket accordingly.

In spite of the incredibly short time that ball and racket are in contact, it is at this moment that the speed, direction and spin of the ball are determined. It follows from this that the choice of racket strings is just as important as that of the frame. At one time racket strings were invariably made of gut – a material produced from cow or sheep intestines. But now, thanks to the advent of artificial fibres, synthetic strings are also available. Both have their pros and cons.

Natural strings are more elastic and absorb the vibrations better, so they are far preferable for players who are liable to develop tennis elbow. Synthetic strings are much less sensitive to rain, and are generally less expensive too.

The thinner the string, the more elastic it will be. This means that it can be more tightly strung without losing its elasticity. But a thinner string will also snap more easily. So when deciding how your racket should be strung, bear the following in mind: fairly loose stringing gives the ball more speed, but tighter stringing provides for better control of the ball. Only you can choose whether speed or accuracy is more important to you. In practice a compromise is usually the answer, which is what most professionals prefer.

Whether or not you are a beginner, however, if you are always suffering from arm or elbow problems you should change to looser strings.

The ball
All that remains is to consider the ball. Some balls are pressurised, while others are without extra internal pressure. An unpressurised ball lasts better and retains its qualities for longer, but is heavier and less elastic. The result is a less lively ball that appears to lack bounce.

Players nowadays use yellow balls almost exclusively, simply because they are easier to see – an important consideration, given the speed at which today's matches are played.

One final piece of advice: always play with good balls if you possibly can; if you persist in making do with a set of soft, ageing balls, then you are going to have considerable problems at a tournament adjusting to new ones that are fresh and responsive.

How do experts string their rackets?
The table on page 118 gives details (including stringing) of the rackets used by participants in the German International Tennis Championships in Hamburg. Here, for the sake of comparison, are the equivalent details of the rackets used by Boris Becker and Steffi Graf at the 1985 Wimbledon Championships: Boris used a "Puma Vilas" frame strung with "VS Mid" strings to a tension of 25 kilos; Steffi used a "Dunlop Max 200 G" strung with "VS Mid" strings to a tension of 29 kilos.

German International Championships, Hamburg, 1985

Name of player	Racket frame	Strings	Tension	RA-frame	RA-strings	Number
Aguilera	Kneissl White Pro	VS 8½	17/17kg	56	55	9
Allen, Trevor	Adidas	VS Top	24/24kg	66	63	12
Arraya, Pablo	Kneissl White Pro	VS 8½	19/18kg	55	57	14
Benhabiles	Kennex Black Ace	Kennex	31/29kg	63	67	8
Bentel, Fidi	Fischer Stan Smith	VS Mid	26/26kg	55	59	2
Birner, Stanislav	Kneissl White Pro	VS 8½	20/19kg	55	61	6
Cancelotti	Donnay Pro 25	VS 9	27/27kg	65	65	2
Casio	Kneissl Aero	VS 9	29/28kg	57	64	8
Castellan	Donnay Pro 25	VS 9	28/28kg	59	65	5
Clerc	Snauwaert Golden Mid	VS 8½	26/26kg	60	68	8
Dyke	Fischer Stan Smith	VS 8½	27.5kg	64	64	1
Elter, Peter	Adidas Magister	VS Mid	22/21kg	64	67	5
Feigl, Peter	Head Edge Edit.	VS 8½	26/25kg	62	61	2
Ganzabal	Dunlop Max 200 G	VS 9	20kg	42	56	4
Garetto		catgut	21/20kg		64	3
Gildemeister, Hans	Dunlop Max 200 G	VS 8½	20/19kg	45	62	17
Gitlin	Wimbledon	VS 9	25/25kg	62	62	4
Günthardt, Heinz	Kneissl White Pro	AFV 8½	22kg	55	63	7
Herrmann, Stefan	Puma Vilas	synthetic	27/25kg	55	64	4
Higueras	Adidas GTM	VS 8½	24/23kg	62	64	3
Hlasek, Jakob	Kneissl White Pro	VS 9	23kg	55	62	6
Ingaramo	Fischer Carbonic	VS 9	20kg	57	55	3
Jaite, Martin	Prince Woodie	VS Top	22kg	43	59	4
Jarryd	Donnay Mid	VS Mid	26/25kg	50	64	5
Keretic	Donnay Diamant	VS 8½	22/21kg	40	63	2
Lewis	Fin Scorpion	synthetic	32kg	50	64	8
Luna, Fernando	Kneissl White Pro	VS 8½	19kg	59	59	5
McNamee	Prince Graphite	VS Top	25kg	57	64	4
Masur	Emrik 2000	VS 8½	30kg	55	64	3
Maurer	Kneissl White Pro	VS Mid	24/23kg	57	67	2
Mecir	Snauwaert Mid	VS 8½	27/26kg	40	64	15
Minussi	Prince Woodie	VS Top	27kg	43	65	2
Mortenson	Donnay Pro 25	VS Top	32kg	53	70	4
Motta	Kneissl White Pro	VS 8½	26kg	55	56	8
Navratil	Kneissl Pro M	VS 8½	24/22kg	52	62	17
Novacek	Kneissl White Mid	VS 8½	27kg	57	66	4
Nyström	Wimbledon	VS 9	25kg	57	60	7
Pecci	Kennex Boron Ace	VS 9	25/24kg	66	61	11
Perez	Snauwaert Mid	VS 8½	23/22kg	60	63	3
Pilic	Puma Blue	VS 8½	24/22kg	40	64	8
Pils	Fischer Mid	VS 9	28/25kg	56	63	3
Pimec	Rossignol F 200	VS 9	25kg	35	64	9
Popp	Snauwaert Mid	VS 8½	25/24kg	52	68	5

Name of player	Racket frame	Strings	Tension	RA-frame	RA-strings	Number
Segarceam	Kneissl White Pro	VS 9	23kg	55	66	1
Simonson, Hans	Dunlop 200 G	VS 8½		46	66	12
Simonson, Stefan	Fischer Carbon	catgut	26kg	50	63	2
Slozil	Kneissl White Star	VS 8½	21/20kg	55	62	13
Sundström	Kennex Boron Ace	VS 9	26kg	62	64	21
Svenson	Fischer Stan Smith	VS Mid	25/24kg	64	63	1
Svenson	Völkl Comp.	VS 8½	22kg	56	60	2
Taroczy	Taroczy	VS 9	23/22kg	62	64	8
Tons	Donnay Boron 25	VS 9	21kg	67	61	1
Vilas	Puma Blue	VS 9	22/20kg	40	59	12
Vojtesch	Kneissl White Pro	VS 8½	22/21	56	59	3
Westphal	Adidas GTX	VS 8½	24/23kg	57	65	6
Wilander	Rossignol F 200	VS 9	22kg	36	61	14
Willenborg	Wilson Ultra 2	catgut	27kg	72	63	2

Adapting to different kinds of court

Tennis courts vary enormously according to the type of surface used, but they are generally classified as "fast" or "slow". Fast surfaces tend to favour a fast, attacking game, while slow surfaces are more suited to the more defensive type of player who feels at home near the baseline. Even among top players, there are very few who feel equally confident on all types of court and have an all-round success rate to match. Moreover, there is now a whole variety of textured synthetic surfaces in addition to the traditional grass and clay courts found all over Europe.

No one can deny that the surface of a court can have a decisive influence on the outcome of a match. This is repeatedly demonstrated in the Davis Cup Tournament, where the host team often inflict some unpleasant surprises on their guests. The hosts first analyse their opponents' game strategies and those of their own team, and lay the kind of surface that they hope will give the opposition the most problems. That, unfortunately, is the way the rules work.

In my opinion, the two most outstanding players who are at home on any court are Rod Laver and Björn Borg. Both have won on the grass courts of Wimbledon as well as on the clay courts of the Roland Garros Stadium in Paris. And while Borg has never actually won the US Championships, he has several times reached the final, even on the synthetic court that is used. These two players have been just as much masters of the fast serve-and-volley game as of the baseline contest that requires so much patience. To be successful on all types of court, a player must be exceptionally well developed physically. Clay courts, for example, require an extraordinary amount of speed if you are going to win.

This is not to say that a baseline strategy is the only means of victory on the slow courts of Paris or Hamburg. On the contrary, players have until recently been far *too* defensive when playing on clay courts; this is mostly due to the fact that the topspin drive has become almost universal as the passing shot used to counter a rush to the net, because it is much less likely to go wrong. You only have to think of those baseline contests in Paris between Mats Wilander the Swede and Guillermo Vilas of Argentina, the results of which owed more to fatigue than to actual technique. But now that Björn Borg's technique has won him victory after victory, there have been plenty who have imitated him.

The fast grass courts of Wimbledon demand a completely different strategy from the clay courts at the Roland Garros Stadium in Paris

Courts made of synthetic materials lead to long tactical rallies but can be hard on the legs

For my part I am convinced that there are ways, even on clay courts, of dealing with these floods of topspin shots. Two methods are in my opinion particularly effective. The first is the slice or chop, which makes the ball bounce so low that a topspin specialist won't have a chance to get his racket under the ball. The second possibility is to hit the ball fast and with relatively little spin. This too can cause problems to a topspin player, because topspin strokes take longer to execute. The result with a fast ball is that ball contact occurs relatively late, and the effectiveness, precision and confidence of the stroke will suffer accordingly. This strategy has always proved effective on faster courts, and I am certain that someone in the future will be able to win with it on clay courts, and will thus put an end to those long, tedious baseline contests.

How can you adapt your game from a slow court to a fast court and vice versa? All you need are a few basic principles that are easily learned. On a fast court, for example, you should shorten the take-back because of the shortage of time available; and in particular you should try to play a more offensive game — even if you are normally happier and more successful when playing from the baseline.

At the other end of the scale, if the court has a tendency to slow the ball down, you must move further in towards the ball to make up for this. Take your time with the take-back and forward stroke, and never hurry them; you will nearly always have time. But the most important thing is never to lose patience! In games on clay courts between equally-matched players, the winner is usually the one who works slowly but surely towards winning the points, and doesn't make the shot until he is absolutely sure of it. Heavy shots aimed directly at the line may occasionally pay off, but will be less successful on average. Finally, tennis on clay courts requires not only patience but fast and tireless footwork. If you can run you will reach every ball. So every time you play on such a court, you must be prepared to work hard without flagging.

There are many players, especially in the spring, who complain about having to switch from indoor to outdoor courts. There are really two factors to consider here: firstly, most indoor courts are faster; and secondly, outdoor courts feel totally different, with the open space, the wind and the sun, and the fact that clay courts are often slippery. There is very little advice that can be given here, except to say that you have to go through with it. The adjustment will obviously be very much easier for a player with a decent technique than for someone who with a bit of bluff can just about manage a serve-and-volley game on a faster court.

But this is something that is true of tennis generally: if you want to achieve lasting success, there are no short cuts. You simply have to learn the strokes. And don't put this off until tomorrow – start now!

The clay centre court at Hamburg

Injuries and their prevention

Sporting activity is great fun and benefits the body physically, but it would be foolish to deny that it also necessarily carries a risk of injury. In tennis, however, the dangers are fortunately fairly slight.

The statistics prove this. Out of the 5,000 amateur sportsmen and women who have been treated for injury at the University Orthopaedic Clinic in Heidelberg, only 4 per cent have actually been tennis players. Of that 4 per cent, two thirds have suffered injuries to the legs, especially to the ankle, the lower leg and knee; and 15 per cent have been injured in the arms and body. By far the commonest complaints (about 40 per cent of cases) have been overuse injuries of the muscles and ligaments. Sprains are the next most common at about 30 per cent, and far behind come fractures, dislocations and torn ligaments. The most commonly affected age group is between 30 and 40, followed by that between 20 and 30. This would suggest that it is often players bordering on the veteran class who expect too much of their bodies (see also the chapter on **Tennis for older players**).

The enormous increase in the number of tennis injuries in recent years is due firstly to the much-increased popularity of the sport, and secondly to the risks which many players have incurred through over-intensive training. It is perfectly understandable that they should wish to emulate the big stars, but they should also reflect on the fact that not everyone is as naturally well built for the game as Boris Becker.

Injury to a professional means loss of earnings, while an amateur loses out on the pleasure of the game; it is undesirable either way. Nowadays, all professional tournaments and institutions have medical and paramedical specialists on hand to provide emergency care. At the Baden Sports Centre in Leimen we work in close cooperation with the University Orthopaedic Clinic in Heidelberg. Here all young players undergo a series of thorough physical examinations. The measures taken as a result of these tests have not only benefitted the health of the players, but have also enabled them to reach a much higher level of technical competence, so that many of them are now to be found among the higher echelons of national and international competition.

Leg and foot problems
As the statistics quoted above show, the lower limbs are particularly liable to injury, especially the feet and the ankles.

Tennis can give rise to injuries, but with appropriate training many of these can be avoided

125

The commonest problems are strains and torn ligaments in the ankles, and strains and torn muscle fibres in the calf and rear thigh muscles, followed by injuries to the knee, in particular to the cartilage and joint capsule. Such injuries are frequently brought about through overuse – especially those in the region of the kneecap itself. Overuse is usually also to blame for foot injuries such as those to the Achilles tendon.

These problems can be caused firstly by the wrong kinds of body movement. All movements should flow smoothly from one to the next. Abrupt, disconnected movements will prove painful and eventually lead to injury. A second contributory factor may be insufficient development of the leg and foot muscles; and the situation may be further exacerbated by inappropriate footwear that doesn't provide enough heel support. Put all three factors together, and injury can practically be guaranteed!

Footwear must be carefully matched to the different court surfaces, especially soft or slippery ones. Many players attempt to provide support for their weak foot and ankle muscles by wearing boots. This is of no help in the long run, since muscles that are already weak will never be encouraged to develop at all. High lace-up boots should only ever be used in those few cases where the ankle keeps keeling over and remains difficult to control even after a hard course of muscular training.

Even amateur players should include the appropriate muscular training in their preparation programme. A few minutes' skipping each day can work wonders. Long-distance running does yet more good, while training in take-off power is especially useful. It is important not to skimp on your training. If you really want to develop extra muscle, then make sure that all movements are carried out smoothly and evenly, and that the hip, knee and ankle muscles are fully stretched. This is the only way of achieving the muscle development and flexibility required.

Trunk problems
Thorough warm-up is essential before every match, carefully warming and stretching every part of the body. You should also bear in mind that the majority of injuries occur as a result of increasing fatigue during the period of activity. Every player knows the symptoms of fatigue, such as backache, stomach and shoulder pain, which he generally puts down to soreness or cramp. But such diagnoses may often be wrong. For it is precisely those areas of the spine, pelvis and shoulder girdle that are liable to the kind of overuse that leads to strained and pulled muscles. These in turn will inevitably lead to restricted movement in every part of the trunk.

Such injuries indicate that at some point a muscle has been overstretched. You might, for example, have bent forwards or backwards while at the same moving sideways or twisting the spine. All these complicated-sounding movements occur naturally during the forehand or backhand, or when serving or smashing the ball. They are simply used to compensate for awkward positioning in relation to the ball, bad reactions or insufficient running speed. The problem is that as the body gets tired it cannot manage these stratagems as efficiently. The answer is better positioning in relation to the ball, quicker reactions and faster running speed. The problem also indicates that you need to pay more attention to developing your stomach and back extensor muscles, especially in the thoracic region of the spine.

The stomach muscles can be strengthened by the following exercise. Lie flat on your back with your knees bent and your feet placed together on the floor. Make sure that your back is completely flat. Now lift your head and upper body simultaneously with your legs so that the two movements balance each other. Continue to raise them until your knees and forehead touch, all the time keeping the movement as smooth and uninterrupted as possible. Then return smoothly and gradually to the starting position, making sure that the small of the back remains in contact with the floor throughout. You can vary the exercise by gripping the muscles at the side of the stomach.

In exercises for strengthening the back muscles, there is nearly always a tendency for any existing hollowness of the back to become exaggerated. In order to avoid this, observe the following procedure. Lie flat on your stomach with your arms stretched forward, and tense up the muscles in your buttocks. Now tense up your stomach muscles, and then gradually lift the whole of your upper body off the ground. If you carry the exercise

out in exactly this fashion, you will not need to hold any additional weights in your hands.

Arm problems

Although a lot is talked about tennis elbow, arm injuries in tennis are less frequent than might be supposed. Tennis elbow is an overuse injury to the tendons of the muscles that control wrist movement. Shoulder problems usually involve overuse injuries to the tendons and joint capsule at the front of the shoulder. Overuse in the wrist area can lead to tendinitis and overstretching of the ligaments and joint capsules.

These injuries are again caused primarily by inappropriate movements, beginning in the area of the shoulder girdle itself. If the shoulder is raised too high, then any movement in the arm will tend to overstretch the muscles in the shoulder, elbow and wrist. As these joints are being twisted at the same time, the tissues will inevitably suffer from overuse. Arm injuries may also be caused by bad positioning, hitting the ball wrongly, and of course an unsuitable racket (see page 115).

The best means of preventing overuse injuries is to use specific exercises to strengthen the muscles involved, including the whole of the shoulder area. The simple press-up is the most useful exercise here. It should be done with the back as stiff as a board and not sagging; the shoulder blades should be flush with the rib cage, and not sticking out like angels' wings; the hands should be turned slightly inwards, and the elbows should never be completely straightened. A series of press-ups should be carried out in a regular rhythm. A variant of the press-up, in which the weight is supported on the fingertips, can be used to strengthen the wrist muscles and the fingers.

Treatment

It is not necessary to go straight to the doctor whenever you feel the slightest twinge. This is particularly true of mild overuse injuries, the pain of which can be easily relieved using ice from the fridge. In changing rooms throughout the world you will see players using ice-bags after matches.

More serious injuries, however, in which the affected area is no longer able to function properly, should be referred for medical treatment as quickly as possible. But even if a damaged limb has to be put in plaster, you should immediately work out a programme for carefully retraining all the muscles as soon as they can be moved freely again. Proper rehabilitation is vital after injury. *Never* return to normal training and competition too soon, or further injury is likely to result.

Boris Breskvar, the coach

It begins as a very ordinary tale. Little Boris bounces a tennis ball against the wall, while his parents play a round of tennis on the court nearby. And then it just so happens that the boy goes to a tennis coach for lessons. He learns how to hold the racket, how to move his legs properly, how to position himself, how to do the strokes, and how to use this enormous racket to hit the ball over a net that is as high as he is tall.

It is still a very ordinary tale as the boy starts to win titles and grows to full stature. He is still learning – and as every pupil and teacher will tell you, it isn't roses all the way. The final part of the story is public knowledge.

The coach who taught him the game has remained behind in that little town of Leimen near Heidelberg. He has long since taken on other pupils, and must observe his one-time protégé from a distance. He is presumably glad and rather proud of the lad; any father, mother, teacher or coach would feel the same. But nobody ever talks of him.

His name is Boris Breskvar. He is a thin, wiry man, with brown hair and merry eyes; he speaks German fluently, but in that rather strange tone that one associates with Yugoslav speakers of German. Breskvar was born in Ljubljana, at a time when things were not exactly easy. Nothing was easy in Europe at the time –

27 August 1942, to be precise. He was the only child of a surgeon. But it was his mother who was interested in sport, as both a rower and a handball player. Boris Breskvar was twelve when he was given his first tennis racket. It was a birthday present; his mother had bought it in Essen in the Ruhr, and it had apparently been made in Pakistan under the trade name of "Evershure".

The Breskvars were a much-travelled family at the time. There was an agreement between West Germany and Yugoslavia involving the exchange of scientific personnel. Thus Breskvar senior worked for many years at a specialist clinic in Heidelberg, and the son divided his time between there and his mother's home in Yugoslavia. He went to school and played tennis – and very well at that. At 14 he was one of the best players in his home province of Slovenia; at 17 he was the best in Yugoslavia. He played in Yugoslavia's King's Cup and Davis Cup teams, which included world-class players such as Pilic, Franulovic and Spear.

A career in tennis, however, seemed out of the question for a left-hander like Boris Breskvar. For three years he studied medicine like his father; but he eventually managed to switch to studying sport, and left college with a coaching diploma. He then wandered around for a few years, playing in Heidelberg, where he was terribly homesick after three months, and Villach in Austria, where he coached Hans Kary.

Then one day in the early 70s he

received a phone call from Ivko Plecevic, the Yugoslavian Davis Cup coach, who in the meantime had settled in Heidelberg. Pleccvic had been offered the chance of promotion, but on condition that he found someone good enough to replace him. Boris Breskvar was taken on as soon as he arrived – first with the *Schwartz-Gelb* ("Black-and-Yellow") club, then with HTC Heidelberg, and later as a coach with the Baden Tennis Association. Two years later he was introduced to a little lad of six at a children's screening session. Boris Becker was his name, and he was to train him for nine years.

Breskvar sees nothing remarkable in the life he has led, and has no regrets. He wouldn't have liked the life of a champion – every day a different hotel and a different stadium to get used to. He prefers to look on, and enjoys it when the young man comes and talks to him. But then he goes back to coaching his new pupils. That's the way it is.

U.K.